3496832?

DIRECTORY

of

IRISH ARCHIVES

Edited by

SEAMUS HELFERTY & RAYMOND REFAUSSÉ

IRISH ACADEMIC PRESS

The typesetting of this book was produced
by Gilbert Gough Typesetting, Dublin,
for Irish Academic Press,
Kill Lane, Blackrock, Co. Dublin.

BRITISH LIBRARY CATALOGUING IN PUBLICATION DATA
Directory of Irish archives.
1. (Republic) Ireland. Archives.
Organisations
I. Helferty, Seamus   II. Refaussé, Raymond
941.7
ISBN 0-7165-2433-3
ISBN 0-7165-2432-5 Pbk

Printed and bound in Great Britain
by A. Wheaton & Co. Ltd, Exeter.

Contents

The American-Ireland Fund

The production of the *Directory of Irish Archives* was assisted by a grant from the American-Ireland Fund.

The Fund was established in 1976 to raise money in the United States of America for the promotion of peace, culture and charity in Ireland. It is opposed to the use of violence. The Fund is non-denominational and non-political serving all Ireland, North and South.

Introduction

Following the successful publication in 1984 of *British Archives,*[1] a new guide to archives in the United Kingdom, the Irish Region of the Society of Archivists (the professional association of archivists in Britain and Ireland) decided to investigate the feasibility of producing a similar guide for Ireland. *British Archives* had been intended as a more comprehensive guide than *Record Repositories in Great Britain,*[2] previously the standard reference work in this field, but it dealt briefly with Northern Ireland and not at all with the Republic of Ireland.

This information gap is given added significance by the under-developed nature of publicly funded archives in Ireland. Unlike the United Kingdom there is no system of county or regional archives while the limited funding of the major repositories in Dublin has prevented them from developing as fully fledged national repositories.

As a result there is a multiplicity of organizations and institutions which to some degree still manage their own archives or which to a limited extent provide a home for other collections on a geographic or thematic basis. Many of these bodies lack the resources to draw to public attention their existence or the material which they hold.

Methods

In 1986 the Irish Region set up a sub-committee to produce a *Directory of Irish Archives.* The members of the sub-committee were Mary Clark, Brian Donnelly, Seamus Helferty, Aideen Ireland, Raymond Refaussé and David Sheehy. Lists of institutions and organizations which were thought likely to hold archives were compiled and their suitability for inclusion assessed. It was decided to exclude certain groups from the *Directory*: trade unions, which are

1 Janet Foster and Julia Sheppard, *British Archives* (London, *1984*).
2 *Record Repositories in Great Britain* (London, Royal Commission on Historical Manuscripts, HMSO, 7th ed., 1982).

the subject of a particular survey by the Irish Labour History Society; business organizations, details of which may be had from the Business Records Survey of the Irish Manuscripts Commission, and family archives, access to which even if they could be detailed, could not be reasonably certain.

In order to ensure that the content of the *Directory* was as current as possible it was decided to proceed by circular rather than by a lengthy series of personal visits, and the work of contacting the various bodies was divided among the members of the sub-committee. Since most of the institutions and organizations to be approached did not have an archivist it was decided to produce as simple a questionnaire as would be consistent with obtaining the basic information which was required. Questionnaires were dispatched in June 1987, the returns were edited during November and December and the script was delivered to the publisher in January 1988.

Apart from the postal address, some explanation may be needed of the other information which is provided:

Telephone number: telephone dialling codes are those which are operative from Dublin.

Enquiries to: since most of the archives do not have permanent salaried archivists, the title of the officer in charge, rather than a personal name has been given.

Opening hours and facilities: it has been assumed that most archives will be closed on public holidays while some, especially academic and religious organizations, may observe more extended closures.

Guides: the criteria for inclusion in this section are that the guide has been published or is an in-house production (e.g. introductory leaflets) for the purposes of general distribution. Since the collections of the more established repositories are detailed in R.J. Hayes, *Manuscript Sources for the History of Irish Civilization* (Boston, 1965) and its *First Supplement, 1965-75* (Boston, 1979), *Hayes* has not been repeatedly cited in this section.

Major collections: because of the considerable disparities in the nature and size of Irish archives and in the degree to which their collections are processed, no attempt has been made to impose a uniformity of style or content on this section, other than to ensure

8

that the material included could, even by the extended terms of reference applicable today, be deemed archival (i.e. primary documentary material and on various occasions non-manuscript material related thereto).

Indexes: since there is no significant geographical concentration of archives in Ireland, apart from in Dublin, it seemed most convenient to arrange the entries in the *Directory* alphabetically by title and provide a basic county index for those who required information on regional repositories. A broad based general subject index is also provided.

Acknowledgements
The Irish Region of the Society of Archivists is indebted to many organizations and individuals for their advice and support in producing the *Directory*. The American-Ireland Fund generously provided essential financial support; Irish Academic Press, and especially its managing director, Michael Adams, guided us through the complexities of publishing in an agreeably brisk and affable manner; Janet Foster and Julia Sheppard gave freely of their advice as editors of *British Archives*. The Irish Region is grateful to the Society of Archivists for its encouragement, to all the members of the Region for their contributions and especially to the members of the sub-committee who undertook the administration of the project. But above all the Region is indebted to all the organizations and institutions which responded to our appeals for information, for without their ready co-operation the production of the *Directory* would have been impossible.

Conclusion
The *Directory* makes no pretence to be a totally comprehensive guide to Irish archives. It is rather an introduction to the many scattered locations where primary source material for the study of Irish history can be found. The aspiration is that institutions and organizations which do not appear in the *Directory*, which are not listed in the appendix, or which have not been excluded for the reasons set out above, either have no archives or have deposited them with another institution. However, the editors will be glad to have details of any significant omissions.

9

1   All Hallows College

Address   Grace Park Rd,
               Dublin 9

Telephone   (01) 373745

Enquiries to   Archivist

Opening hours   By appointment. Brief enquiries may be answered by
and facilities   telephone, lengthy enquiries by post

Guides   None

Major collections
Correspondence between Catholic bishops and priests and the College of
All Hallows, 1842- ; correspondence is from Britain, USA, Australia,
New Zealand, India, Mauritius, West Indies, Argentina and South Africa.
The early correspondence, 1842-77, has been microfilmed and is available in
many overseas state and national libraries.

2   Allied Irish Banks plc

Address   45 College St,
               Dublin 2

Telephone   (01) 7754461

Enquiries to   Archivist

Opening hours   By postal enquiry from researchers providing suitable
and facilities   references. Facilities by arrangement

Guides   None

Major collections
La Touche & Co. (1693-1870): small collection of account books and ledgers.
Provincial Bank of Ireland (1825-1966): Board minutes, circulars from head
offices in London and Dublin, personnel registers.
Royal Bank of Ireland (1836-1966): Board minutes, annual accounts, per-
sonnel registers.
Munster Bank Ltd. (1864-85): small collection of banking records.
Munster and Leinster Bank Ltd. (1885-1966): Board minutes, head office
circulars, personnel records.

3   Archbishop Marsh's Library

Address   St Patrick's Close,
Dublin 8

Telephone   (01) 753917

Enquiries to   Librarian

Opening hours and facilities   10.00-12.45, 2.00-5.00, Mon, Wed-Fri; 10.30-12.30, Sat; photocopying; microfilming

Guides   N.J.D. White, *Catalogue of the Manuscripts remaining in Marsh's Library, Dublin* (Dublin, 1913)

Major collections

c. 300 manuscripts relating principally to Irish history and ecclesiastical history. The collection includes manuscripts from the collections of Narcissus Marsh (1638-1713) Archbishop of Armagh, Edward Stillingfleet (1635-99) Bishop of Worcester, Elie Bouhereau, the first keeper of the Library, John Stearne (1660-1745) Bishop of Clogher and Dudley Loftus (1619-95) jurist and orientalist.

4   Ardagh & Clonmacnoise [R.C.] Diocesan Archives

Address   Bishop's House,
Longford

Telephone   (043) 46432

Enquiries to   Archivist

Opening hours and facilities   By appointment. Every effort will be made to meet the needs of researchers by postal enquiry also

Guides   None

Major collections

Ardagh Diocesan Archives contain considerable collections of papers which formed the correspondence of bishops during the 19th century. The papers begin c. 1820, being noticeably incomplete up to 1853. The episcopate of George Conroy is represented by a small collection. The largest collection is that of Bartholomew Woodlock, 1879-95. There is very little material either extant or available after 1895.

5   Armagh County Museum

Address   The Mall East,
Armagh BT61 9BE

Telephone   (080861) 523070

Enquiries to   Curator

Opening hours 10.00-1.00, 2.00-5.00, Mon-Fri; photocopying;
and facilities   photography

Guides   None

Major collections
Armagh Militia records, 1793- .
Charlemont estate papers, 19th century.
T.G.F. Paterson collection: historical and genealogical manuscripts relating
to the north of Ireland, especially Co. Armagh.
Copies of records relating to Co. Armagh: poll book, 1753; hearth money
rolls, 1664; muster roll, 1630; census of Armagh City, 1770; Armagh
Presbyterian Church Registers, 1727-9, 1796-1809; Manor of Armagh
tenants, 1714; Charlemont estate leases, 1750-1829.

6   Armagh [R.C.] Diocesan Archives

Address   Ara Coeli,
Armagh BT61 7QY

Telephone   (080861) 522045

Enquiries to   Diocesan Secretary

Opening hours By appointment only; reference required;
and facilities   photocopying

Guides   None

Major collections
Correspondence and other papers of Archbishops of Armagh, 1787-1927.
Baptismal records (computerised only) of the diocese to 1900.

7   Bank of Ireland

Address   Head Office,
Lr Baggot St,
Dublin 2

Telephone   (01) 615933

Enquiries to   Secretary

Opening hours   By postal enquiry initially;
and facilities   photocopying

Guides   None

Major collections
Minutes of Board meetings, 1783- ; minutes of annual general courts,
1783- ; original charter and bye-laws; annual reports and accounts, 1783- .

8   Belfast Central Library

Address   Royal Ave,
Belfast

Telephone   (084) 243233

Enquiries to   Irish and Local Studies Librarian

Opening hours   By appointment;
and facilities   photocopying

Guides   *Guide to the Irish and Local Studies Department* (Belfast,
1979)

Major collections
F. J. Bigger (1863-1926): 40,000 items. F. J. Bigger wrote and researched on
local historical topics. He was editor of the *Ulster Journal of Archaeology*,
but his interests were wide ranging and included all aspects of Belfast
history, also the United Irishmen, later nationalist movements and the
revival of the Irish language. The collection includes his own
correspondence and also correspondence collected by him.
J. S. Crone (1858-1945): 10,000 items. J. S. Crone was President of the Irish
Literary Society in London, he was also founder and first editor of the

Irish Book Lover and author of the *Concise Dictionary of Irish Biography*. The collection reflects these interests.

A. S. Moore (1870-1961): 1,000 items. Cuttings, pamphlets, indexes and compilations on local history, with special emphasis on industry.

A. Riddell (1874-1958): 5,000 items. Cuttings, indexes and compilations on social history and local biography.

9   Carlow College

Address	St Patrick's College, Carlow
Telephone	(0503) 31114
Enquiries to	Archivist
Opening hours and facilities	By appointment only; photocopying
Guides	None

Major collections

The archives house part of the College Library collection, particularly materials relating to Bishops of Kildare and Leighlin, to diocesan history, and to notable past students of Carlow College.

Microfilmed account books can be consulted at the National Library, Dublin; this is the main source on early students of the College, 1793- .

10   Carlow County Heritage Society

Address	Scots/Methodist Churches, Athy Rd, Carlow
Telephone	(0503) 42399
Enquiries to	Curator
Opening hours and facilities	By appointment only; photocopying

Guides	None

Major collections
Records of births 1690-1900, marriages 1690-1900 and deaths 1860-1987 for
   Co. Carlow.
Tombstone inscriptions.
Purcell papers, 18th century- .

11   Cashel [R.C.] Diocesan Archives

Address	Archbishop's House, Thurles, Co. Tipperary
Telephone	(0504) 21512
Enquiries to	Archivist, St Patrick's College, Thurles, Co. Tipperary (q.v.)
Opening hours and facilities	By appointment, but originals are made available only in exceptional circumstances. Researchers are advised to consult the microfilm copies of the documents in the National Library, Kildare Street, Dublin. Permission is required to consult the material but is readily given to bona fide researchers. Alternatively, facilities are provided to read the microfilm copies of the documents in St Patrick's College, Thurles; photocopying
Guides	Calendars of the papers in Cashel Diocesan Archives are provided both in the National Library and in Thurles. Some of these have been published by Revd Mark Tierney in *Collectanae Hibernica* 9, 13, 16-20. Other material from the archives has been published by Revd Mark Tierney in *Collectanae Hibernica* 11 and 12 and by Revd Christopher O'Dwyer in *Archivium Hibernicum* xxxiii and xxxiv.

Major collections
Cashel Diocesan Archives contain large collections of the papers of the
Archbishops of Cashel since the early 18th century. These papers are an
important source for the history of the archdiocese of Cashel as well as
containing much material of national interest. The archives contain only a

small number of items which are pre-18th century. The material is catalogued under the names of the various Archbishops of Cashel since the 18th century. Presently the archives are accessible up to the death of Archbishop Croke in 1903.

12   Castle Matrix

Address	Rathkeale, Co. Limerick
Telephone	(069) 64284
Enquiries to	Director
Opening hours and facilities	By appointment or by postal enquiry
Guides	None

Major collections

Castle Matrix is the headquarters of the International Institute of Military History and of the Heraldry Society of Ireland. The archives include: papers relating to the Irish 'Wild Geese' in the service of France and Spain, including a contemporary map of the Battle of Fontenoy and the order of battle 1745, 1690-1820. Heraldic manuscripts including the 1572 Ordinary of Arms of Robert Cooke (Clarencieux King of Arms) comprising over 10,000 coats of arms.

Military archives including the papers of the rocket scientist Dr Clarence N. Hickman and papers relating to the air war in Europe and the Pacific, 1939-45.

13   Cavan County Library

Address	Farnham St, Cavan
Telephone	(049) 31799
Enquiries to	Co. Librarian

Opening hours and facilities	11.00-1.00, 2.00-5.00, Mon-Fri; photocopying
Guides	Sources for Cavan Local History, *Breifne*, 1977-8. Guide to County Cavan Local Studies Department

Major collections

Charter of the town of Cavan, James I, 1610; copy charter of the town of Belturbet by George III; copy charter of the town of Cavan by James II, 28 February 1688.

Farnham Estate papers.

Maps of drainage and navigation of Ballinamore/Ballyconnell, passing from Lough Erne to the Shannon, 1846.

Collection of legal documents, leases, rentals, wills, for Co. Cavan, 18th and 19th century.

Registers, account & fee books, inspectors reports from Bailieboro Model School, 1860s-1900s.

Board of Guardian minute books, 1839-1921.

Rural District Council minute books, 1899-1925.

Newspaper cuttings from national and provincial newspapers on the '2nd' or 'New Reformation' in Cavan, with lists of those who conformed to the established Church, 1824-6. Speeches and posters relating to the 1826 election in Cavan (microfilm).

Diary of Randal McCollum, Presbyterian Minister, Shercock, Co. Cavan, describing social conditions, 1861-71.

Photographs: Eason collection; Valentine collection; miscellaneous photographs and postcards relating to Co. Cavan, 20th century.

14   Chester Beatty Library and Gallery of Oriental Art

Address	20 Shrewsbury Rd, Dublin 4
Telephone	(01) 692386/695187
Enquiries to	Librarian and Director
Opening hours and facilities	10.00-5.00, Tue-Fri, 2.00-5.00, Sat; photocopying; photography; microfilming; photocopying of manuscripts is not allowed

18

Guides   A list of publications available for sale can be obtained
from the Library

Major collections

The collection was the private library of Sir Alfred Chester Beatty
(1875-1968), bequeathed on his death to the Irish people. The manuscript
collection dates from several thousand years B.C. to the 20th century.

Manuscript holdings include:

Cuneiform clay tablets from the Berens collection.

Egyptian papyri: hieratic papyri containing love poems from c. 1160 B.C. and
a finely preserved Book of the Dead of the Lady Neskons.

Greek papyri include those collected by Wilfred Merton and the famous
Biblical Papyri, eleven codices in all, 2nd-4th century A.D.

Among the Coptic papyri are the texts of the lost books of the Manichaen
faith and several biblical texts. There are small collections of Hebrew,
Samaritan, Coptic and Syriac vellum manuscripts, mostly biblical. Among
the Syriac is a 5th century commentary on the Diatessaron by St Ephraim.

There is a small but significant collection of Western manuscripts, including
a 12th century Walsingham Bible and several fine Books of Hours. The
Slavonic manuscripts, also primarily biblical, are notable for their quality
and illumination.

There are over 3,000 Arabic manuscripts in the collection covering every
branch of religious and secular literature. The collection of Qurans
includes a large number of early examples, including a 9th century
example written in gold on blue vellum and a unique Quran written at
Bagdad in 1001 by Ibn al-Bawwab, a celebrated calligrapher. The Persian
manuscripts cover the whole range of painting, calligraphy and book arts
and include a fine 14th century Shah-Namah.

The Indian section has many finely illustrated manuscripts in the Mughal
style, including a chronicle of Akbar the Great. There are several Jain,
Nepalese, Tamil, Kanarese and Sinhalese manuscripts.

The Burmese, Siamese, Tibetan and Mongolian collections number c. 350
items and there are more than 40 Batak manuscripts from Sumatra,
dealing mainly with magical subjects. The Chinese collection contains
more than 170 hand-painted scrolls and albums, and 14 imperial jade
books. In the Japanese collection there are c. 100 scrolls and albums.

The Library also holds Chester Beatty's correspondence relating to the
formation of the collection and the establishment of the Library c. 1910- .

19

15   Church of Ireland College of Education, Research Area

Address	Upper Rathmines Rd, Dublin 6
Telephone	(01) 970033
Enquiries to	Honorary Keeper
Opening hours and facilities	By appointment. Normally materials can only be made available during academic term time. Please write for details and an application form; photocopying; photography
Guides	*Report on the records of the Society for Promoting the Education of the poor in Ireland* [Kildare Place Society] (London, Royal Commission on Historical Manuscripts, HMSO, 1982)

Major collections

Kildare Place Society Collection: central administrative and financial records of the society; general, committee, parliamentary, publishing and inspectors' correspondence; correspondence between the Society and its schools; educational effects.

Church of Ireland Training College Collection: records of the College, 1884-, and some earlier records of the Church Education Society training institution. (Certain classes and ages of documents are closed to researchers).

Other manuscript collections: Disestablishment correspondence, 1860s; Protestant Defence Association correspondence; Kildare Place Ex-Students Association in Northern Ireland collection, 1936-79.

Older printed book and textbooks: copies of textbooks and chapbooks published by the Kildare Place Society in the early 19th century, including those published in tablet or chart form, and a wide range of later 19th and early 20th century Irish textbooks.

16   Clogher [R.C.] Diocesan Archives

Address	Bishop's House, Monaghan
Telephone	(047) 81019
Enquiries to	Archivist
Opening hours and facilities	11.00-1.00, Mon-Wed
Guides	Microfilm and catalogue in Public Record Office of Northern Ireland (q.v.)

Major collections
Papers of James Donnelly, Bishop of Clogher (1864-93).
Baptismal and marriage records for parishes of the diocese to 1880.

17   Convent of Mercy

Address	Carysfort Park, Blackrock, Co. Dublin
Telephone	(047) 761349
Enquiries to	Archivist, Convent of Mercy, Lower Baggot St, Dublin 2
Opening hours and facilities	By arrangement or by postal enquiry; photocopying
Guides	None

Major collections
Letter and papers of the foundress, Mother Catherine McAuley, 1778-1831. Rules and Constitutions, manuscript and printed, with modifications and documents of approval from the Holy See. Register of sisters, 1831-1971. Letters and papers of sisters, 1848-1984. Correspondence with prelates. Records of Mothers General and Council to 1960. Acts of Chapter, 1842-1980.

18 Convent of Mercy, Elphin

Address   St Peter's,
                     Athlone,
                     Co. Westmeath

Telephone   (0902) 92546

Enquiries to   Archivist

Opening hours   Postal enquiry only;
and facilities   photocopying

Guides   None

Major collections
Material relating to the history of the congregation, 1846- , and to individual
    houses, formation houses, schools, orphanages, hospitals and missions.
    Includes annals, theses, correspondence with bishops and with Rome,
    financial records, legal documents, photographs, maps and plans.

19 Convent of Mercy, St Mary's

Address   Bishop St,
                     Limerick

Telephone   (061) 44268/43790

Enquiries to   Archivist

Opening hours   By appointment or by postal enquiry
and facilities

Guides   None

Major collections
Annals of the Sisters of Mercy since their foundation in Limerick, 1838- .
Early registers of the House of Mercy. Early financial accounts. Books
published by Sisters of Mercy. Illuminated register and hand-painted books.
Prayer books and items of clothing. Original letters of Mother Catherine
McAuley and early members of the Community.

20 Coras Iompair Eireann

Address   Heuston Station,
                     Dublin 8

Telephone   Postal enquiries

Enquiries to   Registrar

Opening hours   9.00-5.00, strictly by appointment; photocopying. Access
and facilities   is normally only granted to PhD students

Guides   None

Major collections
Minute books, and Committee minute books of the main constituents of
C.I.E., 1840s —. Thirty-year rule applies.

21 Cork Archives Institute

Address   Christ Church,
                     South Main St,
                     Cork

Telephone   (021) 277809

Enquiries to   Archivist

Opening hours   10.00-1.00; 2.30-5.00 Mon-Fri;
and facilities   photocopying

Guides   Introductory leaflet

Major collections
Record holdings relate to all aspects of Cork history. These include official
  transfers of records from Cork Corporation, Cork County Council, and
  various Urban District Councils, and records of defunct organisations
  such as the Boards of Guardians. Non-offical records include donations
  of business, estate, family, labour and church records.
The chief Corporation collections include minute books of the Borough
  Council, 1901-67; Committee minutes, 1878-1926; Town Clerk's files,
  1920-32. County Council deposits include Council minute book,
  1898-1966; County Secretary's files for 1927; Board of Guardian minute

books for most Cork towns, including an extensive collection of records relating to the Cork City Poor Law Union. The Youghal Corporation records, 1610-1840 are also housed at the Cork Archives.

Among the non-official deposits are the records of: Beamish and Crawford Brewery, 1787-1956; Cork Distillers, 1795-1960; Cork Butter Market, 1793-1904; Cork Coopers Society, 1870-1968. Church records include Holy Trinity Parish (Christ Church) records, 1643-1857, Cork Presbyterian Congregation, Princes Street subscription books, 1758-1822.

Family and estate papers include material relating to the Colthurst Estates in Blarney; the Newenham Estate at Coolmore, Carrigaline and Egmont and other North Cork estates.

Literary collections include manuscripts of James Sheridan Knowles (1784-1862) and Canon P.A. Sheehan (1852-1913).

22   Cork Harbour Commissioners

Address   Harbour House,
                 Custom House St,
                 Cork

Telephone   (021) 273125

Enquiries to   Secretary

*Opening hours   By appointment only;
and facilities* photocopying

Guides   None

Major collections
Minutes of Board meetings, 1814- ; registers of arrivals and sailings, 1912- ; Board members attendance books, 1913- ; registers of conveyances, 1836-1927; bye-laws, 1822- ; accounts, 1871- ; pilotage licences, 1924- .

23   Cork Public Museum

Address   Fitzgerald Park,
                 Mardyke,
                 Cork

Telephone   (021) 270679

Enquiries to	The Curator
Opening hours and facilities	11.00-5.00, Mon-Fri; 9.00-11.00, by appointment
Guides	None

Major collections
A large collection of documents and photographs, 1900-22 including the Mac
Curtáin and MacSwiney papers.

24   Cork-Ross [R.C.] Diocesan Archives

Address	Diocesan Office, Bishop's House, Redemption Rd, Cork
Telephone	(021) 501717
Enquiries to	Diocesan Archivist
Opening hours and facilities	Postal enquiry only; photocopying
Guides	None

Major collections
Correspondence and papers of Bishops of Cork, 1763- .
Annals of the diocese by Dean Dominick Murphy.

25   Corporation of Drogheda

Address	Fair St, Drogheda, Co. Louth
Telephone	(041) 33511
Enquiries to	Town Clerk
Opening hours and facilities	9.00-5.00, by appointment; photocopying

Guides   None

Major collections
Charters: James II, 1687; William III, 1697; George I, c. 1725; William IV, 1833.
Council Book (Minutes), October 1649- .
Freedom Books, 1690- .
Maps: Newcomen's map of Drogheda, 1657; Ravell's map of Drogheda, 1749; Skinner and Taylor's map of Drogheda, 1778; Greene's map of Drogheda, 1878.

26 Corporation of Sligo

Address	Town Hall, Sligo
Telephone	(071) 42141/2
Enquiries to	Town Clerk
Opening hours and facilities	9.00-1.00, 2.00-5.00, Mon-Fri; photocopying
Guides	None

Major collections
Minutes of Sligo Corporation meetings, 1842-1941; register of premises (Explosives Act, 1875), 1879-1916; register of music performed in Town Hall, 1938-46; register of public entertainments (Town Hall), 1930-48; minutes of artisans & housing committees, 1886-1920; lists of burgesses of Sligo Borough, 1868-1906; Sligo Cemetery Trust ledger, 1868-86; valuation & rate books, 1842- .

27 County Museum

Address	The Castle, Enniscorthy, Co. Wexford
Telephone	(054) 35926
Enquiries to	Hon. Secretary

Opening hours and facilities	10.00-6.00, June-Sept; 2.00-5.30, Feb-May, Oct-Nov
Guides	None

Major collections
Letters, maps, deeds, miscellaneous papers referring mostly to the 1798 and 1916 rebellions in Co. Wexford.

28 Crawford Municipal Art Gallery

Address	Emmet Place, Cork
Telephone	(021) 273377
Enquiries to	Gallery Secretary
Opening hours and facilities	10.00-5.00, Mon-Fri; by appointment; photocopying; photography
Guides	None

Major collections
The library contains the remnants of the School of Art library, dating from the mid-19th century, including many large portfolios on architecture and the decorative arts. Minute books of the Technical Instruction Committee (later the Vocational Education Committee), incomplete student registers, 19th-20th centuries.

29 De Valera Library and Museum

Address	Harmony Row, Ennis, Co. Clare
Telephone	(065) 21616
Enquiries to	Librarian
Opening hours and facilities	11.00-5.30, Mon, Wed, Thurs; 11.00-8.00, Tues, Fri; photocopying; photography; microfilming

Guides	Catalogue of Poor Law Records

Major collection:
Poor Law records of Co. Clare, 1850-1922; Grand Jury Presentments, 1854-1900; minute book of the Borough of Ennis, 1699-1810.

30   Donegal County Library County Archive Centre

Address	The Courthouse, Lifford
Telephone	(074) 21968 (temporary)
Enquiries to	Librarian
Opening hours and facilities	By appointment; photocopying; photography
Guides	Calendar of Boards of Guardians minute books

Major collections
Boards of Guardian records for Ballyshannon, Carndonagh, Donegal, Dunfanaghy, Glenties, Letterkenny, Milford and Stranorlar, 1840s-1923.
Minutes of County Council committees; miscellaneous Council records.
Small collection of private records including estate papers.

31   Down & Connor [R.C.] Diocesan Archives

Address	73a Somerton Rd, Belfast BT15 4DJ
Telephone	(084) 773935
Enquiries to	Archivist
Opening hours and facilities	Postal enquiry only; photocopying;
Guides	None

Fr William McMullan correspondence, 1803-09.
Bishop Cornelius Denvir correspondence, 1835-65.
Archbishop William Crolly of Armagh correspondence, 1835-49.
Bishop Daniel Mageean correspondence 1929-62.

32   Down, Connor & Dromore Diocesan Library

Address	Talbot St, Belfast
Telephone	None
Enquiries to	Hon. Secretary
Opening hours and facilities	By appointment
Guides	J.R. Garstin 'Descriptive Catalogue of the Bishop Reeves Collection of Manuscripts' in *Down and Connor and Dromore Diocesan Library Catalogue of Books . . .* (Belfast, 1899)

Major collections

Notebook and account books of Francis Hutchinson (Bishop of Down and Dromore 1720-39).

Miscellaneous correspondence of Lord John George Beresford (Archbishop of Armagh 1822-62) relating mainly to the dioceses of Down and Connor.

Manuscripts of William Reeves (Bishop of Down and Connor 1886-92) relating mainly to Irish Church history and antiquities.

Calendar by Reeves of the Armagh primatial registers of Archbishops Octavian, Cromer, Swayne, Prene, Mey.

Clerical succession lists and genealogical papers of Canon H.B. Swanzy (1873-1932).

Miscellaneous records of Church of Ireland societies and organizations in the dioceses of Down and Connor.

33   Drogheda Harbour Commissioners

Address   Harbour Office,
The Mall,
Drogheda

Telephone   (041) 38378/36026

Enquiries to   Secretary

Opening hours 9.30-5.30, Mon-Fri;
and facilities   photocopying; photography

Guides   None

Major collections
Minute books, 1790- .

34   Dromore [R.C.] Diocesan Archives

Address   Bishop's House,
Newry,
Co. Down

Telephone   (080693) 2444

Enquiries to   Bishop of Dromore

Opening hours Access by special request only;
and facilities   photocopying;

Guides   None

Major collections
Correspondence and papers of bishops, 1770- .
   Records of baptisms, marriages and deaths for each parish, 1926- .
   Other diocesan and parish papers.

35   Dublin Corporation Archives

Address   City Hall,
Dame St,
Dublin 2

Telephone   (01) 796111 (ext. 2818/9)

Enquiries to   Archivist

Opening hours   10.00-1.00, 2.15-5.00, Mon-Fri; by appointment;
and facilities   photocopying; photography; microfilming

Guides   Introductory leaflet; Mary Clark, *The Book of Maps of the Dublin City Surveyors 1695-1827* (Dublin, 1983)

Major collections

Royal Charters of the City of Dublin (102 items), 1171-1727; medieval cartularies, including Liber Albus and Chain Book of Dublin; Dublin City Assembly Rolls, 1447-1841; minutes of Board of Aldermen of Dublin, 1567-1841; minutes of Sheriffs and Commons of Dublin, 1746-1841; Tholsell Court of Dublin, 16th-18th century; Dublin City Treasurer's Accounts, 1540-1841; Freedom Records, 1576-1918; City Surveyor's Maps, 1695-1827; archives of Wide Streets Commission, 1757-1849; archives of Paving Board, Dublin, 1774-1840; Mansion House Committee for Relief of Distress in Ireland, 1880; records of townships and of Urban District Councils, of Rathmines and Rathgar, 1847-1930; of Pembroke, 1863-1930; and of Howth, 1918-40. Minutes of Dublin City Council, 1841-1930; photographic collection of the Liffey Bridges, 1880s; records of Dublin Corporation committees and departments, 1840-1930.

36   Dublin Corporation Gilbert Library

Address   138-141 Pearse St,
Dublin 2

Telephone   (01) 777662

Enquiries to   Librarian

Opening hours and facilities	10.00-1.00, 2.15-5.30, Mon-Thurs; 10.00-1.00, 2.15-4.45, Fri and Sat; photocopying; photography; microfilming
Guides	Douglas Hyde & D.J. O'Donoghue (comps), *Catalogue of the Books & Manuscripts comprising the Library of the Late Sir John T. Gilbert* (Dublin, 1918)

Major collections

286 manuscripts and transcripts of manuscripts, collected by, or transcribed for, Sir John T. Gilbert in connection with his work on the history of the City of Dublin and on Irish history. The Robinson MSS, c.1740-60, the notebooks and other documents of an Irish judge, are of interest in that they deal with notable law cases in which Mr Justice Robinson was involved; the collection of letters addressed to Richard Caulfield, 1848-60, cover topics connected with Irish topography and genealogy; James Goddard's 'Complete abstract of Deeds belonging to the Guild of St Anne' includes material on Dublin parishes and trade guilds. Transcripts include the Assembly Rolls of Dublin, 1660-1803, charters and documents of the Guild of the Holy Trinity or Merchant Guild of Dublin 1438-1824, and other guilds of the city; and a transcript of the Book of Charters belonging to the City of Dublin. Some transcripts are of documents which have since been destroyed or disappeared (e.g. copies of letters on state affairs in Ireland, from the Phillipps Collection — the originals were destroyed in a fire in 1711).

37   Dublin [R.C.] Diocesan Archives

Address	Archbishop's House, Drumcondra, Dublin 9
Telephone	(01) 379253
Enquiries to	Archivist
Opening hours and facilities	10.00-1.00, 2.00-5.30, Mon-Fri; prior appointment is essential; photocopying
Guides	Calendars of the collections are available until 1860. Calendars of the papers of Archbishop Murray (1823-52) have been published in *Archivium Hibernicum* xxxvi-xlii. For a general overview see David C. Sheehy, 'Dublin Diocesan Archives — an introduction', *Archivium Hibernicum* xlii (1987)

Major collections
Papers of the Roman Catholic archbishops of Dublin, c. 1750- .
Papers of bishops (auxiliary), priests and lay persons, 1820- .
Diocesan (Chapter) records, 1729- .
Minutes of meetings of bishops, 1829-49; 1882.
Combined surviving records of the Catholic Board, the Catholic Association and the Repeal Association, 1806-47.
Papers of Dr Bartholomew Woodlock, rector of the Catholic University, 1854-79.
Records of Holy Cross College, Clonliffe, 1867-1946.

38   Dundalk Harbour Commissioners

Address	Quay St, Dundalk
Telephone	(042) 34096
Enquiries to	Secretary
Opening hours and facilities	By appointment only; photocopying; photography
Guides	None

Major collections
Minute books, 1844- (some gaps); miscellaneous account books, 1850s- ; wages books, 1908- ; arrivals books, 1916- .

39   Dunsink Observatory

Address	Dublin 15
Telephone	(01) 387911/387959
Enquiries to	Director
Opening hours and facilities	Postal enquiry/appointment; photocopying; photography
Guides	None

DIA—C

Major collections
Miscellaneous astronomy documents, 1790-1850. Correspondence, minutes, 1947-87, held at Dublin Institute for Advanced Studies, 10 Burlington Road, Dublin 4

40   Elphin [R.C.] Diocesan Archives

Address	Diocesan Office, St Mary's, Sligo
Telephone	(071) 62670
Enquiries to	Diocesan Secretary
Opening hours and facilities	By appointment; photocopying
Guides	None

Major collections
Correspondence of Bishops Laurence Gillooly, John Clancy, Bernard Coyne, Edward Doorly and Vincent Hanly, 1858-1970. Some historical data on parishes in Elphin Diocese.

41   Fermanagh County Museum

Address	Castle Barracks, Enniskillen, Co. Fermanagh
Telephone	(080365) 25050 (ext. 244)
Enquiries to	Museum Officer
Opening hours and facilities	9.00-1.00, 2.00-5.00, Mon-Fri; photocopying; photography
Guides	None

Major collections
Local Government: Co. Fermanagh criminal book, 1861-1969; landholding and sales posters; County Assize proclamations.

Education: Parish of Derrymacausey primary school register, 1844-54.
Genealogy: correspondence of Lady Dorothy Lowry-Corry, 1931-5; family
    records of Canon W.H. Dundas (d. 1941).
17th Century Documents: appointment of Hamilton as Governor of Ennis-
    killen, 1689; letter from Schomberg to Wynne, 1689; commission of Major
    J. Folliott as major in the Dragoons, 1689.
Ephemera dealing with entertainment, sport, politics, religion and or-
    ganizations in Co. Fermanagh.

42   Franciscan House of Studies

Address   Dun Mhuire,
                Seafield Rd,
                Killiney, Co. Dublin

Telephone   (01) 826760

Enquiries to Archivist

Opening hours By appointment or postal enquiry;
and facilities photocopying

Guides   G.D. Burtchaell and J.M. Rigg, *Report on Franciscan
                Manuscripts preserved at the Convent, Merchants' Quay,
                Dublin* (Dublin, Royal Commission on Historical
                Manuscripts, 1906).
                C. Mooney OFM, 'Franciscan Library, Killiney: a short
                guide', *Archivium Hibernicum* xviii (1955), 150-6.
                Myles Dillon, Canice Mooney OFM, Padraig de Brun,
                *Catalogue of Irish manuscipts in the Franciscan Library,
                Killiney* (Dublin, 1969).

Major collections
Irish manuscripts, 12th century- ; Irish Franciscan Continental Colleges,
17th-19th century; Franciscan friaries in Ireland, 17th-20th century;
Wadding Papers, 17th century; non-franciscan Irish material, 17th-20th
century; Hayes Papers on the Veto Question, early 19th century; vellum
codices in Latin comprising works by non-Irish Franciscans on theology and
philosophy, 15th-17th century.

43   GPA-Bolton Library

Address   John St,
                  Cashel,
                  Co. Tipperary

Telephone   (062) 61944

Enquiries to Custodian

Opening hours 9.30-5.30, Mon-Sat; 2.30-5.30, Sun. A better service can
and facilities   be provided if prior notice is given

Guides   None

Major collections
Church of Ireland archives relating to parishes in the Cashel-Dundrum
    Tipperary-Aherlow quadrilateral, 17th century -, including Chapter
    minute books from c. 1780.
Miscellaneous ecclesiastical and secular manuscripts, with title deeds and
    legal documents, manuscript maps, plans, diaries, research notes, and
    writings, together with photographs, late 19th century- .

44   Galway County Libraries

Address   Island House,
                  Cathedral Square,
                  Galway

Telephone   (091) 62471/7039

Enquiries to Executive Librarian

Opening hours 9.30-1.00, 2.00-5.00, Mon-Fri;
and facilities   photocopying

Guides   None

Major collections
Estate papers: O'Kelly of Castlekelly; Blakes of Ballyglunin; some
    encumbered estates material.
Board of Guardian minutes: Tuam Union, 1839-1921.
Rural District Council minutes: Ballinasloe, 1909-18; Clifden, 1899-1925;
    Gort, 1899-1924; Galway, 1904-21; Mountbellew, 1899-1913; Portumna,

1900-25; Tuam, 1917.

Galway Hospital minutes and accounts, 1892-1922; Galway Co. Board of Health minutes, 1922-39; Clonbrock Dispensary minutes, 1852-98.

45 Galway [R.C.] Diocesan Archives

Address   The Cathedral,
              Galway

Telephone   (091) 63566

Enquiries to   Archivist

Opening hours 10.00-5.00, Mon-Fri
and facilities

Guides   None

Major collections

Matters dealing with Galway Diocese.

Documents and correspondence in relation to the Diocese of Galway, Kilmacduagh and Kilfenora.

46 Galway Harbour Commissioners

Address   49 Dock St,
              Galway

Telephone   (091) 62329/61874/63738/64750

Enquiries to   Secretary

Opening hours 9.30-5.30, Mon-Fri; photocopying. University College
and facilities Galway (q.v.) holds microfilm copies of Galway Harbour
              Commissioners records which may be consulted with
              written permission from the Commissioners.

Guides   None

Major collections

Minute books, 1833- ; arrivals and departures book, 1872-1901; tonnage and imports dues book 1884-1914; export dues book, 1882-1914; general maintenance and wages ledger, 1830-67; printed abstracts of accounts, 1854-1934.

47   Genealogical Office

Address	2 Kildare St, Dublin 2
Telephone	(01) 611626/614877
Enquiries to	Chief Herald
Opening hours and facilities	10.00-12.30, 2.30-4.30, Mon-Fri; photocopying; photography; microfilming
Guides	None

Major collections

Registers of arms, 16th century- .

Registrations of pedigrees, 16th century- .

Heraldic visitations, mainly of Cos. Dublin and Wexford, 16th-17th century.

Sixteen volumes of funeral entries, 17th century.

Lords' Entry volumes (records relating to the introduction of peers to the Irish House of Lords), 18th century.

Records of the Order of St. Patrick (founded 1783).

Records of Sir William Beetham especially his abstracts from Irish prerogative wills (30 volumes) and pedigrees (23 volumes).

Commissioned genealogical searches, 19th-20th century.

48   General Register Office/ Oifig An Ard-Chláraitheora

Address	Joyce House, 8/11 Lombard St East, Dublin 2
Telephone	(01) 711000 (ext. 339/320)
Enquiries to	Ard-Chláraitheoir Cúnta
Opening hours and facilities	9.30-12.30, 2.15-4.30, Mon-Fri; photocopying
Guides	Oifig An Ard-Chláraitheora list of records

Major collections

Registers of births registered in all Ireland, 1 Jan 1864 - 31 Dec 1921, and in Ireland (exclusive of the six north eastern counties) from that date.

Registers of deaths registered in all Ireland, 1 Jan 1864 - 31 Dec 1921, and in Ireland (exclusive of the six north eastern counties) from that date.

Registers of marriages in all Ireland from 1 Apr 1845 - 31 Dec 1863, except those celebrated by the Roman Catholic clergy.

Registers of all marriages registered in the whole of Ireland, 1 Jan 1864 - 1 Dec 1921, and in Ireland (exclusive of the six north eastern counties) from that date.

Note: Only the indexes to the above records are open to public inspection, on payment of appropriate fee. Clients may purchase copies of individual entries identified in the Index.

49   General Register Office

Address	Oxford House, 49/55 Chichester St, Belfast BT1 4HL
Telephone	(084) 235211
Enquiries to	Deputy Registrar General
Opening hours and facilities	9.30-3.30, Mon-Fri; photocopying; photography; microfilming
Guides	Information leaflets

Major collections

Records of births and deaths held in the General Register Office relate mainly to those registered since 1 Jan 1864 in that part of Ireland which is now Northern Ireland.

Marriage records are available in this office from 1922 only.

For information on a marriage which occurred subsequent to civil registration and prior to 1922 application should be made to the District Registrar, addresses of whom are obtainable from the General Register Office.

General searches are not undertaken by the office staff. The indexes are made available to the applicant or his appointed representative.

50   Geological Survey of Ireland

Address	Beggars Bush, Haddington Rd, Dublin 4
Telephone	(01) 609511
Enquiries to	Public Office
Opening hours and facilities	Public office 2.30-4.30: other times by appointment; photocopying; photography;
Guides	Typed lists available on request

Major collections

Geological Survey of Ireland field sheets: original six-inch to the mile (1:10, 560) geological field maps of the 26 counties, 1845-87 and early 20th century six-inch glacial drift/land use maps of Cork, Dublin and Limerick city areas.

Geological Survey of Ireland archives: miscellaneous manuscripts from the Portlock Survey, 1820s-40s; Geological Survey of Ireland correspondence books, 1845-c.1900; du Noyer geological drawings, 1836-69; and printed material — reference set of geological maps of Ireland (largely 19th century) and pre-1900 geological books, from the Geological Survey library and the Portlock Bequest.

51   Glenstal Abbey

Address	Murroe, Co. Limerick
Telephone	(061) 386103
Enquiries to	Archivist
Opening hours and facilities	Postal enquiry only
Guides	None

Major collections

Non-monastic: Carbery papers, 1658-1759; Sir Thomas Hackett papers, 1688-1720; Cloncurry papers, 1880-1909; correspondence between

Mother Mary Martin and Bede Lebbe, 1930s; Fr John Sweetman papers, 1911-23; diaries of Richard Hobart, 1784-1802, Sir Thomas Kane,1837, and J. Grene Barry, 1869-76; Gaelic League Ard-Craomh minute book, 1907-15.

Monastic: foundation correspondence; legal and administrative documents; financial, farm and school records; seniorate minute books, 1927-80; material relating to congresses, 1952- ; material relating to the foundation in Nigeria, 1974- .

52 Grand Lodge of Ancient, Free & Accepted Masons of Ireland

Address   17/19 Molesworth St,
Dublin 2.

Telephone   (01) 761337/609328

Enquiries to   Librarian & Archivist

Openings hours Mon-Fri; by appointment only;
and facilities photocopying; photography; microfilming

Guides   None

Major collections

Grand Lodge records: membership registers of 2,300 lodges and minute books of various administrative bodies. Correspondence files relating to Irish Masonic lodges at home and overseas, early 18th-20th century.

Subordinate Lodge records: minute books and other effects of individual lodges (c. 300 individual collections).

Records of Masonic benevolent institutions including the records of the Masonic Female Orphan School (founded 1792) and the Masonic Boys' School (founded 1867). Charity Petitions, 18th-20th century. Restricted access.

Microfilms and photocopies of Irish Masonic records held in other custodies, 18th-20th century.

53   Guinness Museum

Address St James' Gate,
Dublin 8.

Telephone (01) 756701 (ext. 528)

Enquiries to Curator

Openings hours 9.15-4.00, Mon-Fri; by appointment only;
and facilities photocopying;

Guides None

Major collections
Minute books of the Brewers' Guild of Dublin, 1759; Brewers' Corporation, 1805; Coopers' Guild of Dublin, 1765-1836. The charter of the Coopers' Guild is also in the collection.

54   Holy Ghost Congregation (Irish Province)

Address Temple Park,
Richmond Ave South,
Dublin 6

Telephone (01) 975127/977230

Enquiries to Archivist

Openings hours By appointment only;
and facilities photocopying;

Guides None

Major collections
The collection goes back to the origins of the Congregation in Ireland in 1859.

55   Honourable Society of King's Inns

Address Henrietta St,
Dublin 1

Telephone (01) 747134

Enquiries to Librarian

Openings hours 2.00-6.00, Mon; 11.00-6.00, Tue-Fri; 10.00-1.00, Sat;
and facilities During academic year Library opens 2.30-6.00, Mon and
2.30-9.00, Tue-Thur, otherwise hours as above. Library
closes for month of July. Researchers should write in advance stating nature of their enquiry; photocopying

Guides Padraig de Brun, *Catalogue of Irish Manuscripts in King's
Inns Library Dublin* (Dublin Institute for Advanced
Studies, 1972); Edward Keane, P. Beryl Phair and Thomas
U. Sadleir, *King's Inns Admission Papers, 1607-1867*
(Dublin, Irish Manuscripts Commission, 1982); T. Power,
'The "Black Book" of King's Inn: an introduction with an
abstract of contents', *The Irish Jurist* xx (1985), 135-312.

Major collections

Archives of the Society, 1607-1917, which include the 'Black Book'
1607-1730, Bench Minutes, 1792-1917, admission records of barristers,
and admission records of attorneys up to 1866.

29 Irish language manuscripts, the majority dating from the 18th century, but
five of which were written as early as the 1400s.

Private paper collection of John Patrick Prendergast (1808-1893).

Manuscripts of Bartholomew Thomas Duhigh (c.1750-1813), Assistant
Librarian to the Society.

Manuscript parliamentary journals and miscellaneous legal manuscripts.

56   Incorporated Law Society of Ireland

Address Blackhall Place,
Dublin 7

Telephone (01) 710711

Enquiries to Librarian

Openings hours and facilities	9.00-5.00, Mon-Fri; by appointment only; photocopying
Guides	None

Major collections
Minute books of meetings of Council, 1922-.

57   The Irish Agricultural Museum

Address	Johnstown Castle Old Farmyard, Wexford
Telephone	(053) 42888
Enquiries to	Curator
Openings hours and facilities	By appointment only; photocopying
Guides	None

Major collections
Small amount of mill account books and estate records, mostly from Co.
   Wexford, c. 1850-1900.
Machinery manufacturers' catalogues, 1900-50.

58   Irish Architectural Archive

Address	63 Merrion Square, Dublin 2
Telephone	(01) 763430
Enquiries to	Director
Openings hours and facilities	10.00-1.00, 2.00-5.00, Mon-Fri; photocopying; photography
Guides	None

Major collections
Extensive collection of photographs of Irish buildings of all types and periods
   from medieval times to the present day.

Original architectural designs and copy drawings, 18th-20th century.
Records from architects and surveyors; biographical index of architects,
19th-20th century.

59 Irish Christian Brothers (Northern — St Mary's — Province)

Address	Christian Brothers' Provincialate, 274 North Circular Rd, Dublin 7
Telephone	(01) 300247
Enquiries to	Archivist or Revd Brother Provincial
Openings hours and facilities	Not open but postal enquiries attended to; photocopying;
Guides	None

Major collections
Material relating to the history, evolution and administration of the
Congregation. Material relating to St Mary's Province, 1956-.

60 Irish Film Institute

Address	6 Eustace St, Dublin 2
Telephone	(01) 795744
Enquiries to	Director
Openings hours and facilities	By appointment or postal enquiry; photocopying
Guides	None

Major collections
The collection contains some 550 Irish films, principally documentaries of
the 1940s and 1950s.

61   Irish Jesuit Archives

Address   35 Lr Leeson St,
Dublin 2

Telephone   (01) 761248

Enquiries to   Archivist

Openings hours By appointment only
and facilities

Guides   Fergus O'Donoghue SJ, 'Irish Jesuit Archives',
Archivium Hibernicum xli (1986), 64-71

Major collections
Administrative material, including correspondence with the Generalate of
the Order; personal papers of distinguished Jesuits; manuscripts of books
and sermons; retreat notes, papers relating to property; photographs; rare
books by Irish Jesuits; manuscripts in Irish. Original manuscripts cover the
period 1575-1960. Transcripts cover the period 1540-1774. In late 1986 much
20th century material, including papers relating to Irish Jesuit missions in
Australia, Hong Kong and Zambia, was transferred to the archives.

62   Irish Jewish Museum

Address   3/4 Walworth Rd,
South Circular Rd,
Dublin 8

Telephone   None

Enquiries to   Archivist

Openings hours 11.00-3.30, Mon, Wed, Sun, May-Sept; 10.30-2.30, Sun,
and facilities   Oct- Apr. Other times by appointment

Guides   None

Major collections
Minute books and records of various communal institutions and synagogues,
registers of births, marriages and deaths, correspondence and communal
publications, 1820-.

63   Irish Railway Record Society

Address   Heuston Station,
                Dublin 8

Telephone   (01) 528428

Enquiries to   Archivist

Openings hours   8.00-10.00, Tue; by appointment
and facilities

Guides   Joseph Leckey, *The records of the Irish Transport Genealogical Archive*. Occasional Publication No. 7 of the Irish Railway Society (Belfast, 1985); Joseph Leckey and Peter Rigney, *IRRS Archival Collections D1-D10* (Dublin, 1976); Joseph Leckey, *The Records of the County Donegal Railways* (Belfast, 1980)

Major collections

Transport archives, 18th century- , including waterways, roads, and air transport, but predominantly railways. Private collections and non-current archives of CIE, the national transport undertaking.

Incorporates Irish Transport Genealogical Archive: the personal records of transport employees, 1870s-1950s as far as these have been located. Fine collection of transport and other directories.

Ordnance Survey maps covering much of the railway system, with 200,000 other maps and drawings, largely unsorted.

Most complete collection of Parliamentary plans of Irish railways outside House of Lords Record Office. Other books of plans include docks, drainage, tramways, reservoirs, markets, and hotels as well as contractors' plans of railways.

64   Irish Rugby Football Union

Address   62 Lansdowne Rd,
                Dublin 4

Telephone   (01) 684601

Enquiries to   Secretary

Openings hours and facilities	By appointment; photocopying
Guides	None

Major collections
Minute books, miscellaneous papers, photographs, press cuttings, memorabilia, 1874-.

65 Irish Theatre Archive

Address	c/o Archives Division, City Hall, Dublin 2
Telephone	(01) 796111 (ext. 2818/9)
Enquiries to	Honorary Archivist
Openings hours and facilities	10.00-1.00, 2.15-5.00, Mon-Fri; by appointment; photocopying; photography; microfilming
Guides	Articles in *Prompts: Bulletin of the Irish Theatre Archive* nos. 1-6 (1981-3)

Major collections
Extensive collections of ephemera, including programmes, posters, playbills, photographs, scrapbooks, press-cuttings and prompt-books, relating to theatres, amateur groups and theatre clubs, especially in Dublin, 1850- .
Victorian and Edwardian picture-postcards of theatrical figures.
Archives of the Irish Theatre Company, 1975-83; Dublin Theatre Festival, 1959-; Brendan Smith Academy, 1950-80.
Original costume and stage designs, including Michael Mac Liammoir and Wendy Shea.
Memorabilia of Jimmy O'Dea (1899-1965) and Shelah Richards (1903- 85).
Collection of unpublished plays (typescript) including Lennox Robinson, Patrick Kavanagh, John Mac Donagh.

66   James Joyce Museum

Address   Joyce Tower,
               Sandycove,
               Co. Dublin

Telephone   (01) 809265/808571

Enquiries to   Curator

Openings hours and facilities   10.00-1.00, 2.00-5.00, Mon-Sat, May-Sept, Oct-Apr; by appointment

Guides   None

Major collections
Letters and papers (mostly photocopies), portraits, photographs, printed ephemera and personal possessions of James Joyce (1882-1941).

67   Kerry County Library

Address   Moyderwell,
               Tralee,
               Co. Kerry

Telephone   (066) 21200

Enquiries to   Co. Librarian

Openings hours and facilities   10.30-5.30, Mon-Sat; photocopying; microfilming

Guides   None

Major collections:
Board of Guardian records.
Minute books: Cahirciveen, 1905-22; Dingle, 1840-1920; Glin 1870-91; Kenmare, 1840-1921; Killarney, 1840-1923; Listowel, 1845-1922; Tralee 1845-1922.
Rough Minute books: Dingle, 1849-1921; Killarney, 1840-71; Listowel, 1856-99; Tralee, 1845-1922.
Rural District Council minute books: Caherciveen, 1900-25; Dingle, 1899-1925; Kenmare, 1899-1921; Killarney, 1900-25; Listowel, 1901-11; Tralee 1900-25.

Kerry Board of Health records:.
Minute books: Board of Health & Public Assistance, 1930-42; Board of
Health, 1925-31; Board of Health and Labourers' Acts, 1937-42; Board
of Health Tuberculosis Section, 1927-31; Board of Health and Public
Assistance Tuberculosis Section, 1932-42.

68   Kerry [R.C.] Diocesan Archives

Address	Bishop's House, Killarney, Co. Kerry
Telephone	(066) 31168
Enquiries to	Archivist
Openings hours and facilities	By appointment
Guides	None

Major collections
Material connected with episcopates of Nicholas Madgett, Bishop of Kerry
(1753-74) and of each subsequent bishop of the diocese, as well as more
personal papers of several bishops and some priests.

69   Kildare County Library
Local History Dept.

Address	Athgarvan Rd, Newbridge, Co. Kildare
Telephone	(045) 31486
Enquiries to	Assistant Librarian, Local History Dept.
Openings hours and facilities	9.30-1.00, 2.00-5.00, Mon-Fri; photocopying

Major collections
Board of Guardians minute books: Naas Poor Law Union, 1841-1922; Athy
    Poor Law Union, 1914-20; Celbridge Poor Law Union, 1910-19.
Minute books of Kildare Co. Council, 1899-1919.
Grand Jury Presentments, 1810-93.
Rural District Council minute books: Celbridge, 1907-13; Edenderry,
    1899-1919; Naas 1903-21.

70   Kilkenny Corporation Archives

Address   City Hall,
                 High St,
                 Kilkenny

Telephone   (056) 21076

Enquiries to   Town Clerk

Openings hours By appointment or postal enquiry only;
and facilities photocopying

Guides   None

Major collections
Charters, Grants, Letters Patent of the City of Kilkenny, 1170-1862, including
the 1st Charter of Wiliam Earl of Pembroke to the Burgesses of Kilkenny,
1170, and the Charter of James I, 1609, creating Kilkenny a City. Minute
books of the Corporation, including the first minute book, the 'Liber Primus
Kilkennienses', 1231-1538; minutes of the 'Mayor and Citizens' of Kilkenny,
1656-1843; minutes of the 'Mayor Aldermen and Burgesses', 1843-1952;
minutes of various committee meetings, 1892-1938; proceedings of the
Corporation of Irishtown, 1544-1834; minutes of the Kilkenny Urban
Sanitary Authority, 1875-6, 1917-42. Grand Roll of Freeman of the city of
Kilkenny, 1760- . Deeds, conveyances, leases, letters, petitions and
addresses, c. 13th-19th century.

71   Kilkenny County Library

Address   6 John's Quay,
Kilkenny

Telephone   (056) 22021/22606

Enquiries to   Assistant Librarian

Opening hours   10.30-1.00, 2.00-5.00, Mon-Fri; 7.00-9.00, Mon & Wed
and facilities   evenings; 10.30-1.30, Sat; photocopying

Guides   None

Major collections
Local administrative records including Board of Guardian records, 1839-1923; Rural District Council records, 1894-1926; Grand Jury records, 1838-98; Registers of Electors, 1940-78.
Records of Theatre Unlimited in Kilkenny, 1985-6.
Arts Week records donated by Mr R.W. Girdham, former Chairman, 1974-86.
Business records of Clover Meats, Waterford, 1920-80.
200 photographs of Kilkenny City relating to Amenity Study by Bolton St, College of Technology, Dublin, Architectural Faculty, 1970.

72   Kilmainham Gaol Museum

Address   Inchicore,
Dublin 8

Telephone   (01) 535984

Enquiries to   Curator, Pearse Museum (q.v.)

Opening hours   2.00-6.00, Wed & Sat; otherwise by appointment;
and facilities   photocopying; photography

Guides   None

Major collections
A miscellaneous collection of documents, photographs, uniforms, arms and personal effects, 1798-1924. There is a particularly interesting collection of material from the 1916-22 period.

73   Kilmore [R.C.] Diocesan Archives

Address	Bishops's House, Cullies, Cavan
Telephone	(049) 31496
Enquiries to	Archivist, St Patrick's College, Cavan
Opening hours and facilities	By appointment or by postal enquiry
Guides	None

Major collections

Correspondence and papers of bishops including Lenten pastorals, letters to Rome, private office papers, sermons, visitation books, deeds, plans, wills, photographs and press cuttings, 1836- .

Archives of St Patrick's College, Cavan, including rolls, prize lists, deeds, plans and account books, 1869- .

Correspondence and papers of priests of the diocese including the collections of Revd Philip O'Connor, Owen F. Traynor and T.P. Cunningham.

74   Kilrush Urban District Council and Kilrush Harbour Board

Address	Town Hall, Kilrush, Co. Clare
Telephone	(065) 51047/51596
Enquiries to	Town Clerk
Opening hours and facilities	9.30-5.00, Mon-Fri; photocopying
Guides	None

Major collections

Minute books, 1885- ; harbour arrivals and departures books, 1875- ; general maintenance and wages ledgers and printed abstracts of accounts, 1885- .

75   Kinsale Harbour Commissioners

Address   Harbour Office,
Custom's Quay,
Kinsale,
Co. Cork

Telephone   (021) 772503

Enquiries to   Secretary

Opening hours   By appointment only
and facilities

Guides   None

Major collections
Minute books, 1870- ; arrivals and departures books, 1898- ; export and
import books, 1898- ; maps, plans and drawings of the harbour, 1883; cash
books, 1879- ; bye-laws, 1870- .

76   Land Commission, Records Branch

Address   24 Upper Merrion St,
Dublin 2

Telephone   (01) 789211

Enquiries to   Keeper of Records

Opening hours   By appointment;
and facilities   photocopying

Guides   None

Major collections
The documents held by the Land Commission Records Branch are mainly
title documents of estates acquired by the Commission and are the property
of the landlords or their agents. They include:
Abstracts of Title, Title Documents and Maps lodged by Vendors of Estates.
Schedules of particulars of tenancies on the estates.
Orders vesting such estates in the Land Commission.
Records of Proceedings.

Schedules showing particulars of the allocation of the Estate Purchase
Moneys.
Tenants fiated purchase agreements and Fair Rent Orders and Agreements.
Orders and Final Lists vesting holdings in Tenants and resale Maps.
Resumption Orders made by the Commissioners and the Judicial
Commissioner.
Apportionment Orders, Right of Way Orders.
Records of the late Congested Districts Board and of the Church
Temporalities Commission, 17th century-.

77   Laois County Library

Address	County Hall, Portlaoise
Telephone	(0502) 22044
Enquiries to	Co. Librarian
Opening hours and facilities	9.00-5.00, Mon-Fri; by appointment photocopying
Guides	None

Major collections

Queen's Co. (Laois) Co. Council: minute book, 1900-25; rate books, 1916-62;
Barrow drainage scheme, 1939-45; account books, 1930-47; blind welfare
scheme, 1934-52; free milk, 1942-50; tuberculosis comm., 1916-25; road
works, 1929-30; register of cases sent to external hospitals, 1926-58; home
assistance, 1934-53; hospital administration records for Co. Infirmary,
1880-1924; Co. Hospital, 1933-60; Co. Home, 1933-34; Abbeyleix District
Hospital, 1924-57; St Brigid's Sanitorium (Shaen), 1930-61; minute book
and correspondence of Portlaoise swimming pool, 1967-76.
Minutes of Board of Guardians: Abbeyleix, 1844-1919; Donaghmore,
1851-86; Mountmellick, 1845-1920.
Records of Urban District Councils: Abbeyleix, 1909-25; Athy, 1913-25;
Cloneygowan, 1903-23; Mountmellick, 1899-1925; Roscrea, 1905-25;
Slievemargy, 1909-25.
Bye-laws of Maryborough, 1731; Stradbally assizes, 1816-41; tenants account
book, Deerpark, Kilkenny, 1836-46.

78   Ledwidge Museum

Address   Jeanville,
                   Slane,
                   Co. Meath

Telephone   (041) 24336

Enquiries to   Curator

Opening hours   10.00-1.00, 2.00-7.00, Mon-Thur, Sat; 1.00-7.00, Sun
and facilities

Guides   None

Major collections
Poems and memorabilia of the poet Frances Ledwidge, 1887-1917.

79   Leitrim County Library

Address   Ballinamore,
                   Co. Leitrim

Telephone   (078) 44012

Enquiries to   Leabharlannai Contae

Opening hours   10.00-1.00, 2.00-5.00, Mon-Fri;
and facilities   photocopying

Guides   Catalogue of Board of Guardians and Rural District
                   Council holdings

Major collections
Mohill Board of Guardians minute books, 1839-1922; Manorhamilton Board
    of Guardians minute books, 1839-1923; Carrick-on-Shannon Board of
    Guardians minute books, 1843-1919.
Records of Kinlough Rural District Council, 1902-25; Mohill Rural District
    Council, 1899-1924; Manorhamilton Rural District Council, 1899-1925.
Large collection of ledgers and account books from various shops and
    business premises.
Minute books of various committees.

80   Limerick Museum

Address   1 John's Square North,
Limerick

Telephone   (061) 47826

Enquiries to   Curator

Opening hours   Public opening: 10.00-1.00, 2.15-5.00, Tue-Sat; Curator
and facilities   available Mon-Fri, Mon by appointment. Prior notice of
visit advised for enquiries; photocopying; photography

Guides   None

Major collections
Miscellaneous documents, maps, photographs relating to Limerick, c. 17th
century- .

81   Linen Hall Library

Address   17 Donegall Square North,
Belfast BT1 5GD

Telephone   (084) 321707

Enquiries to   Librarian

Opening hours   9.30-6.00, Mon-Fri; 9.30-8.30, Thur; 9.30-4.00, Sat;
and facilities   photocopying; photography

Guides   None

Major collections
Archives of the library, 1791- , including manuscript minutes of the
Governors of the Library; wages books; minutes of various committees.
Manuscript meteorological records for Belfast, 1796-1906.
Joy MSS: selected materials for the annals of the province of Ulster, collected
by Henry Joy, 18th century and early 19th century.
Minutes of the Belfast Literary Society, 1801- .
Minutes of Belfast Burns Society, 1931- .

82   Louth County Library

Address   Chapel St,
Dundalk

Telephone   (042) 35457

Enquiries to   Librarian

Opening hours   10.00-1.00, 2.00-5.00, Tue-Sat;
and facilities   photocopying;

Guides   None

Major collections
Poor Law Guardians minute books: Dundalk, 1839-1924; Drogheda,
1839-1919; Ardee, 1851-1924.
Co. Louth Grand Jury records, 1830-98.
Ardee: Corporation minutes, 1661-1841; Borough Court books, 1746-75;
Clerk of the Court's minute book, 1889-1963; poll book, 1768.
Miscellaneous Co. Louth estate rentals and accounts, 1857-86.
Records of Dundalk Free Library, 1869-1911; Mechanics Institute Library,
1832-57; Dundalk Gas Light Company, 1856-98; Dundalk Premier Utility
Society, 1929-38; Great Northern Railway, 1915-46; Board of
Superintendents of Co. Louth Jail, 1832-62; North Louth Local Defence
Force 1940-1.

83   Mary Immaculate College

Address   South Circular Rd,
Limerick

Telephone   (061) 314923

Enquiries to   Librarian

Opening hours   9.00-10.00, during term time; 9.00-5.00, during vacations;
and facilities   photocopying;

Guides   None

Major collections
Irish Folklore Commission collection.

84   Mayo County Council

Address   Courthouse,
Castlebar

Telephone   (094) 21033

Enquiries to   Co. Secretary

Opening hours   By appointment only; photocopying
and facilities

Guides   None

Major collections
Mayo: minutes of Co. Council, 1900-30; minutes of Co. Board of Health, 1908
and 1926.
Castlebar: minutes of Rural District Council, 1909-17; accounts of Rural
District Council, 1900-18; minutes of Urban District Council, 1900-30.
Ballina: minutes of Urban District Council, 1900-30.

85   Meath County Library

Address   Railway St,
Navan,
Co. Meath

Telephone   (046) 21134/21451

Enquiries to   Co. Librarian

Opening hours   9.30-1.00, 2.00-5.00, Mon-Fri; 10.00-12.30, Sat; 7.00- 8.30,
and facilities   Tue & Thur; photocopying

Guides   None

Major collections
Board of Guardians minute books: Dunshaughlin Union, 1839-1921; Kells
Union, 1839-1922; Navan Union, 1839-1921; Oldcastle Union, 1870-1920;
Trim Union, 1839-1921.
Rural District Councils minute books: Kells, 1899-1923; Navan, 1899-1925;
Dunshauglin, 1899-1925; Ardee, 1899-1925.
Meath Co. Council: minutes, accounts, correspondence, valuation books,
1904-60.

Navan Urban District Council: minutes, accounts, correspondence, 1920-50.
Meath County Library Committee records, 1931- .
Board of Health: minute books 1934-42; Public Assistance record books,
1920-44.
Meath Co. Infirmary, Navan: records, 1809-1960.
Claytons Woollen Mills, Navan: records, 1919-66.

86   Meath Diocesan Registry

Address   Trim,
Co. Meath

Telephone   None

Enquiries to   Diocesan Registrar

Opening hours   By appointment
and facilities

Guides   None

Major collections
Miscellaneous diocesan records, mid 19th century-.
Miscellaneous collection of ecclesiastical manuscripts including manuscripts of Anthony Dopping (Bishop of Meath) relating to Irish Bishop-
rics, 1686; correspondence of Lord John George Beresford (Archbishop
of Armagh, 1822-62), 1820-61; notebooks of Revd W. Reynell (1836-1906)
relating mainly to Meath diocese and clergy, 16th-19th century.

87   Michael Davitt National Memorial Museum

Address   "Land League Place",
Straide,
Co. Mayo

Telephone   None

Enquiries to   Curator

Opening hours   12.30-6.30, Mon-Sat; 2.00-7.00, Sun
and facilities

Guides   Introductory leaflets, guides

Major collections
Miscellaneous papers relating to Michael Davitt (1846-1906): addresses of welcome, 1882-95; letters and cards, 1898-1905; police reports, 1879-82; photographs, 1879-82; diary of the Governor of Dartmoor Prison, 1870-82.

88   Mid West Archives

Address   The Granary,
              Michael St,
              Limerick

Telephone   (061) 40777

Enquiries to Regional Archivist

Opening hours   9.30-1.00, 2.15-5.30, Mon-Fri. Prior notice is advisable, as
and facilities records are held at various locations. Research service
               available for a fee; photocopying; microfilming

Guides   None

Major collections
Poor Law minute books, 1838-1923 and Rural District Council minute books, 1899-1925 for Cos Limerick, Clare and Tipperary.
Limerick Co. Council minute books, 1898- ; Co. Board of Health minute books, 1923-44.
Limerick Corporation: Freedom records, 1737-1905; Council and Committee minute books: 1841- ; Tholsel Court records, 1773-1833.
Commissioners for St Michael's parish: minute books, 1819-44; rate books, 1811-44; night watch reports, 1833-49.
Limerick Chamber of Commerce: minute books, 1807- ; export books, 1815-50.
Limerick Harbour Commissioners: minute books, pilot books, tonnage dues, 1823- .
St John's Hospital: minutes, correspondence, register of patients, accounts, 1816-1905.
Sir Vere Hunt papers, 1716-1818; Monteagle papers, 1605-1930; Coote papers, 1776-1843; miscellaneous deeds from solicitors' collections, 1624-1900.

89   Military Archives

Address	Cathal Brugha Barracks, Rathmines, Dublin 6
Telephone	(01) 975499/975782 (ext. 51)
Enquiries to	Military Archivist
Opening hours and facilities	10.00-4.00, by appointment only
Guides	None

Major collections

Collins papers relating to the formation of the I.R.A., 1919-22.

Liaison papers concerning the period between the Truce and the Civil War, containing correspondence between the Irish and British authorities relating to breaches of the Truce.

Civil War material including operational and intelligence reports from all commands, July 1922-Mar 1924; copies of radio reports between all commands and the Commander in Chief, Adjutant General, Quartermaster General and Director of Intelligence; Railway Protection Corps, Internment Camps, Press and Publicity and Special Infantry Corps files; orders, instructions and memoranda; documents captured from anti-Treaty forces dealing with operational and intelligence matters; Department of Defence files, 1922-5; complete army census, Nov 1922.

Army Crisis, 1924; Army Organisation Board, 1926; Military Mission to U.S.A., 1926-7; Temporary Plans Division, 1928; Volunteer Force files, 1934-9; internees files; minutes of G.H.Q. Staff Conferences, 1925-39.

Director of Intelligence, Director of Operations, Construction Corps, and Air Defence Command files, 1939-45; G.H.Q. unit journals; look out posts log books; minutes of G.H.Q. Conferences and Controller of Censorship files.

Director of Operations, 1945-74; Air Corps and Naval Service; United Nations Service, 1958-84.

Copies of handbooks and military publications including *An t-Oglach* and *An Cosantoir*.

c. 50 private paper collections of former army personnel.

90 Millmount Museum

Address Millmount,
Drogheda,
Co. Louth

Telephone (041) 36391

Enquiries to Curator

Opening hours 3.00-6.00, Tue-Sun. Also by appointment
and facilities

Guides None

Major collections
Millmount Museum: catalogue of contents.
Drogheda Union (Board of Guardians): minutes, accounts, register of
    children, 1858-1923.
River Boyne Company: journal 1790-5.
Drogheda Rowing Club: minute book, 1895-1914.
Drogheda Carpenters and Joiners' Society: minute book, 1867- .
Drogheda Brick and Store Layers' Society: account book, 1895- 1948.

91 Missionary Sisters of the Holy Rosary

Address Generalate House,
23 Cross Ave,
Booterstown, Co. Dublin

Telephone (01) 881708

Enquiries to Archivist

Opening hours 10.00-5.30, Mon-Fri, by appointment;
and facilities photocopying

Guides None

Major collections
Correspondence and documents relating to the foundation of the
Congregation, 1920-4. Official documents, reports and correspondence with
the Congregation for Religious (Rome), with ecclesiastical authorities and

with Mission Houses. Private correspondence of members of the congregation, including letters of the founder, Bishop Shanahan. Community annals covering the opening of all missions and their development. General records of the administration and growth of the congregation. Circular letters. Bulletins, newsletters and magazines. Biographical material/necrologies.

92   Monaghan County Museum

Address	The Hill, Monaghan
Telephone	(047) 82928
Enquiries to	Curator
Opening hours and facilities	10.00-1.00, 2.00-5.00, Mon; by appointment; photocopying
Guides	None

Major collections

Papers from various estates, mostly in Co. Monaghan but also in Co. Louth and Co. Dublin, 18-20th century.

Marron collection of extracts from records relating to Co. Monaghan in the Public Record Office, London; State Paper Office, Dublin; Marquis of Bath's archives in Longleat House, Wiltshire.

Monaghan County Council: minutes, rate books, ledgers, 1899-1959.

Miscellaneous records of Monaghan Urban District Council, Clones Petty Sessions, Monaghan Co. Infirmary, Castleblayney Workhouse, 19th-20th century.

Legal papers relating to the Local Authority (Labourers Act).

Small collections of papers of Charles Gavan Duffy (1816-1903) and Senator Thomas Toal, 1911-42.

93   Mount Melleray Abbey

Address	Cappoquin, Co. Waterford
Telephone	(058) 54404

Enquiries to	Librarian
Opening hours and facilities	Postal enquiry only
Guides	None

Major collections
Cistercian antiphoner, 12th century. Cistercian graduale. Latin Vulgate version of the Bible, 13th or 14th century. Collection of Irish manuscripts.

94 National Botanic Gardens

Address	Glasnevin, Dublin 9
Telephone	(01) 374388/377596/371636/371637
Enquiries to	Director
Opening hours and facilities	By appointment only; photocopying
Guides	None

Major collections
Official correspondence of the Director, c. 1870- .

Moore papers: family papers, official documents relating to Dr David Moore and Sir Frederick Moore, c. 1838-1922 (photostat copies).

Augustine Henry papers: annotated books, manuscripts, notebooks (including tree books of Henry J. Elwes), Chinese diaries, 1880-99, annotated proofsheets of Elwes' & Henry's *Trees of Great Britain and Ireland*, 1880-1930.

Botanical correspondence of Natural History Section of National Museum (transferred to National Botanic Gardens in 1970); principal correspondents are N. Colgan, R.L. Praeger, R.A. Phillips and J. Muir.

Watercolours: extensive collection of over 1500 original watercolours of plants cultivated in the Botanic Gardens, 1880-1920, by Lydia Shackleton, Josephine Humphries, Alice Jacob; watercolours of European plants by the Hon. Frederica Plunkett & the Hon. Katherine Plunkett, c. 1880; c. 400 pen-and-ink sketches of Irish plants by S. Rosamond Praeger (original drawings for books by Robert L. Praeger, her brother), c. 1900.

Accessions books: records of plants donated to and distributed from the Gardens, 1834- .

Wages books and staff records, c. 1860- .

Photographs: uncatalogued collection of glass-plate negatives taken of the Botanic Gardens, c. 1910-40 (c. 5,000 items).

C.F. Ball photographs: collection of photographs taken in Bulgaria and France while collecting plants, c. 1910.

Headfort papers: miscellaneous papers about the garden at Headfort House, Kells, Co. Meath including documents about the formation of the arboretum at Headfort, c. 1914.

95   National College of Art and Design

Address	100 Thomas St, Dublin 8
Telephone	(01) 711377
Enquiries to	Librarian
Opening hours and facilities	9.30-5.15, Mon, Fri; 9.30-9.15, Tue, Wed, Thur; photocopying; photography
Guides	None

Major collections

Records of all enrolled students, 1877-1940. Post 1940 records are available elsewhere in the College.

Newspapers cuttings relating to Irish art and design, c. 1985- .

Exhibition catalogues, invitations to gallery openings and ephemera relating to 20th century Irish art and design.

96   National Gallery of Ireland Library

Address	Merrion Square, Dublin 2
Telephone	(01) 615133 (ext. 109)
Enquiries to	Librarian
Opening hours and facilities	10.00-5.30, Mon-Fri

Guides   None

Major collections
National Gallery Archives: Gallery papers from the foundation in the 1860's.
Manuscript material on some artists; manuscript material relating to the
provenance of paintings in the collection.

97   National Library of Ireland

Address   Kildare St,
                Dublin 2

Telephone   (01) 765521

Enquiries to   Director

Opening hours   Manuscript Reading Room: 10.00-12.40, 2.00-5.15,
and facilities   6.15-9.00, Mon-Thur; closes 5.15 pm Fri, 1.00 pm Sat;
                photocopying, photography; microfilming

Guides   General information in leaflet *Use of the National Library.*
                Gaelic manuscripts: *Catalogue of Irish manuscripts in the
                National Library of Ireland* (Dublin, Dublin Institute for
                Advanced Studies, 1967-). Major accessions noted in
                annual *Report of the Council of Trustees of the National
                Library of Ireland.*

Major collections
c. 1100 Gaelic manuscripts including 100 from the Phillipps collection, 14th
    century- .
c. 100 major estate collections including Ormonde of Kilkenny Castle,
    Devonshire of Lismore Castle, Headfort of Headfort House.
Literary papers including those of W.B. Yeats, Maria Edgeworth and Patrick
    Kavanagh.
Political papers including those of Roger Casement, William Smith O'Brien,
    Daniel O'Connell, Patrick Pearse, John Redmond.
Labour and trade union papers including those of Thomas Johnson and
    William O'Brien.

98   National Museum of Ireland

Address	Kildare St, Dublin 2
Telephone	(01) 765521
Enquiries to	Librarian
Opening hours and facilities	10.00-5.00, Tue-Fri; by appointment; photocopying; photography
Guides	None

Major collections
Correspondence relating to the administration of the Museum and the acquisition of items now in the collections. Archives of the Natural History Museum including notebooks and journals of naturalists whose collections are held by the Museum, 1850- .

99   New Ross Harbour Commissioners

Address	Harbour Office, New Ross, Co. Wexford
Telephone	(051) 21303
Enquiries to	Secretary
Opening hours and facilities	9.00-5.30, Mon-Fri; photocopying
Guides	None

Major collections
Minute books, 1848-1986; shipping books, 1958- ; letterbooks and correspondence, 1927-40, 1980- ; register of vessels, 1848-91; register of mortgages, 1851-76; ledgers, 1848-1900 and other financial records.

100   Offaly County Library

Address   O'Connor Square,
Tullamore

Telephone   (0506) 21113/21419 (ext. 211)

Enquiries to   General Office

Opening hours   By appointment;
and facilities   photocopying

Guides   Catalogue of local authority records

Major collections
Board of Guardians minute books: Birr, 1910-15; Edenderry, 1879-1919;
Parsonstown, 1839-1921; Tullamore, 1839-1921.
Rural District Council minute books: Birr, 1899-1928; Edenderry, 1913-28;
Kilbeggan, 1889-1918; Roscrea, 1899-1917; Tullamore, 1899-1917.
King's Co. Council: accounts, personal ledgers, letters, hospital and Co.
Infirmary records, 1837-1964.

101   Office of Public Works

Address   51 St Stephen's Green,
Dublin 2

Telephone   (01) 613111

Enquiries to   Information Officer

Opening hours   9.15-5.30, Mon-Thur; 9.15-5.15, Fri
and facilities

Guides   None

Major collections
Records of most public works in Ireland, 1831- , including construction of
public buildings, relief schemes, arterial drainage and marine works.
Record of the Archaeological Survey and the Sites and Monuments record
of Ireland.

102 Oireachtas Library

Address   Leinster House,
                  Kildare St,
                  Dublin 2

Telephone   (01) 789911

Enquiries to   Librarian

Opening hours   Admission to the Library is normally restricted to members
and facilities of the Oireachtas and Oireachtas officials. Members of the
                  public will only be admitted by permission of the Ceann
                  Comhairle [Speaker]. Access should then be arranged with
                  the Librarian; photocopying

Guides   None

Major collections
Manuscripts records of trials conducted by the Special Commission
(Fenianism), 1866.
Miscellaneous reports on aspects of Irish affairs including ports, gaols, public
records and the work of public offices, 17th-19th century.

103 Ordnance Survey of Ireland

Address   Phoenix Park,
                  Dublin

Telephone   (01) 213171

Enquiries to   Assistant Director

Opening hours   9.30-12.15, 1.15-4.30, Mon-Fri. Appointment by postal
and facilities enquiry only; photography; microfilming

Guides   None

Major collections
Mansucript drawings of the original 6 inch survey of Ireland (Fair
Plans), c. 1829-41, by parishes, and the O'Donovan name books for all
townland names contained within the parishes. Town-plans for various
towns in the Republic of Ireland surveyed on different scales but largely
on 5 inch to 1 mile, c. 1829-41. All other material and documents which
went into the production of these maps. Progress returns from some of

the districts involved in the Survey.

All manuscripts and documents relating to the 25 inch Survey of the Republic, c. 1888-1911 (c. 1863- , Dublin only). Levelling books, contour cards, revised cards, field traces, trig distance and description books..

Miscellaneous maps (pre Ordnance Survey) and books from the Down Survey, c. 1650- .

104   Ossory [R.C.] Diocesan Archives

Address   Sion House,
Kilkenny

Telephone   (056) 21060

Enquiries to   Bishop of Ossory

Opening hours   By appointment only;
and facilities   photocopying

Guides   None

Major collections
Papers and correspondence of bishops and priests, 1639- .

105   Pearse Museum

Address   St Enda's Park,
Rathfarnham,
Dublin 14

Telephone   (01) 934208

Enquiries to   Curator

Opening hours   All year ex. Dec 25 & 26; 10.00-12.30 daily; 2.00-3.30,
and facilities   Dec-Jan; 2.00-4.30, Feb & Nov; 2.00-5.30, Mar-Apr &
Sept-Oct; 2.00-6.00, May-Aug; photocopying

Guides   None

Major collections:
Documents, photographs and personal effects relating to Patrick Pearse (1879-1916) and the history of St Enda's.

106 Public Library

Address Abbey St,
        Armagh BT61 7DZ

Telephone (0871) 523142

Enquiries to Keeper

Opening hours 2.00-4.00, Mon-Fri. Closed mid July — end of Aug
and facilities

Guides *Catalogue of Manuscripts in the Public Library of Armagh*,
        1928

Major collections

Papers of Anthony Dopping, Bishop of Meath (1682-97) relating to the
    diocese of Meath.

Correspondence of Lord John George Beresford, Archbishop of Armagh
    (1822-62).

Papers of William Reeves, Bishop of Down (1882-96) relating to Irish church
    history from the 5th to the 19th century.

Records of 17th and 18th century episcopal visitations.

Copies of Armagh primatial registers, 1362- .

107 Public Record Office of Ireland

Address Four Courts,
        Dublin 7

Telephone (01) 733833

Enquiries to Deputy Keeper

Opening hours 10.00-5.00 Mon-Fri; photocopying; photography;
and facilities microfilming

Guides *Short Guide to the Public Record Office of Ireland (1964).*
        Reports of the Deputy Keeper of the Public Records in Ireland
        nos. 1-59 (1869-1962);.
        The Public Record: Sources for local studies in The Public
        Record Office of Ireland (1982).
        Information leaflet 'Sources for genealogy and family
        history'; information leaflet 'Sources for medieval history'.

Major collections

The Public Record Office receives court and probate records 20 years after their creation, and also has responsibility for pre-disestablishment parish registers of the Church of Ireland. The National Archives Act, 1986, provides for the transfer of records of government departments and offices when they are more than 30 years old. Some departments (including Agriculture, Foreign Affairs, Finance, Justice) have already transferred records to this office. In addition the PRO receives records from many private sources including firms of solicitors, estate offices, charities, trade unions and private individuals. The following is a selective list of accessions from official sources, all of which are available for research.

Board of Health, Cholera Papers, 1932-4.

Census Returns, 1901 and 1911.

Chancery Pleadings, 16th-18th century.

Commissioners of National Education, 1832-1924.

Companies Registration Office, files of dissolved companies to 1953.

Custom and Excise, establishment and administration papers, 1778-1837.

Department of Agriculture, 1899-1954.

Exchequer and plea rolls, 14th-15th century.

Incumbered Estates Court, Landed Estates Court and Chancery Land Judges rentals, 1850-82.

Irish Record Commission, 1810-30.

Office of Public Works, 19th - early 20th century.

Prison Registers, 19th-20th century.

Quit Rent Office, 17th-19th century.

Relief Commission, 1845-7.

Royal Hospital, Kilmainham, 1684-1929.

Shipping agreements and crew lists, 1863-1922.

Tithe Applotment books, 1828-37.

Valuation Office and Boundary Survey, 19th century.

108   Public Record Office of Northern Ireland

Address	66 Balmoral Ave, Belfast BT9 6NY
Telephone	(084) 661621

Enquiries to	Director
Opening hours and facilities	9.15-4.45, Mon-Fri; annual closure first 2 weeks in Dec; photocopying; photography; microfilming
Guides	*Reports of the Deputy-Keeper of the Records*; Sectional lists on the textile industry records, landed estate records, church registers, maps and plans. Introductory leaflet, *A Guide to the Public Record Office of Northern Ireland*.

Major collections

Records of Northern Ireland Government Departments, Courts and Public
Bodies, mainly from 1921, but also including some 19th century records
such as the Ordnance Survey maps, copy wills, the tithe applotment books,
valuation records, the records of the Boards of Guardians, school
registers and records of the Commissioners of National Education.

Private records: estate and family papers, business and solicitors' records,
emigrant letters, the records of private societies and organisations, copies
of church records.

109   Queen's University of Belfast

Address	Main Library, Queen's University, Belfast BT7 1NN
Telephone	(084) 245133 (ext. 3607)
Enquiries to	Special Collections Department
Opening hours and facilities	9.00-1.00, 2.00-5.00, Mon, Thur, Fri; 9.00-1.00, 2.00- 9.00, Tue, Wed. Open mornings only during Aug; photocopying; photography;
Guides	South and South East Asian material noted in M.D. Wainright, *A guide to Western manuscripts and documents in the British Isles relating to South and South East Asia* (London, 1965). Chinese material noted in N. Matthews, *A guide to manuscripts and documents in the British Isles relating to the Far East* (Oxford, 1977). Australian material noted in P. Mander Jones, *Manuscripts in the British Isles relating to Australia, New Zealand and the Pacific*

(Canberra, 1972). African material noted in N. Matthews, *A guide to manuscripts and documents in the British Isles relating to Africa* (Oxford, 1971). Mary T. Kelly (comp.), *Papers of Helen Waddell: a calendar* (1981).

Major collections
Archives of the University, 1909- , and of its predecessors, Queen's College, 1845-1909, Queen's University in Ireland, 1850-82, and the Royal University of Ireland, 1881-1909.

Scientific papers and correspondence of Thomas Andrews, 1828-76, and James Thomson, 1857-92.

Musical manuscripts collected and compiled by Edward Bunting, 1792-1943. Original works by Sir Hamilton Harty, 1900-39.

Literary manuscripts of Arthur O'Shaughnessy, c.1863-70; Edith Somerville and Violet Martin, 1873-1948; Helen Wadell, 1909-50; Shan Bullock, 1889-1935.

Correspondence and classical and other papers of R.M. Henry, 1899-1941.

Personal papers of Sir Robert Hart, Inspector General of the Chinese Imperial Maritime Customs, 1854-1908, and of Stanley F. Wright, Commissioner of the Chinese Imperial Maritime Customs, 1850-1951.

110   Raphoe [R.C.] Diocesan Archives/ Cartlann Ratha — Bhath

Address	Monastery Ave, Letterkenny, Co. Donegal
Telephone	(074) 36122
Enquiries to	Archivist
Opening hours and facilities	Postal enquiry only; photocopying
Guides	None

Major collections
The archives, only recently established, is in the process of formation. It is essentially the episcopal archives, beginning with Bishop James McDevitt (1870-9). Papers of Bishops Daniel McGettigan, Michael Logue and Patrick O'Donnell are being acquired from Armagh Diocesan Archives (q.v.).

111 Registry of Deeds

Address	Henrietta St, Dublin 1
Telephone	(074) 733300
Enquiries to	The Registrar
Opening hours and facilities	10.00-4.30, Mon-Fri; photocopying
Guides	Margaret Dickson Falley, *Irish and Scotch-Irish Ancestral Research* (2 vols.). P.B. Eustace (ed.), *Registry of Deeds. Abstract of Wills vol i, 1708-45* (Dublin, 1956). Do. *vol ii, 1746-85* (Dublin, 1954). Eilish Ellis & P.B. Eustace (eds), *vol iii, 1785-1832* (Dublin 1984)

Major collections
Records of registered deeds of transfer of ownership or interest in property, 1708- , records of wills, 1708-1832. Some records of marriage settlements. This office maintains an index of names of grantors, 1908- , and an index of placenames, 1708-1947, to all our records.

112 Religious Society of Friends Historical Library

Address	Swanbrook House, Morehampton Rd, Donnybrook, Dublin 4
Telephone	(01) 687157
Enquiries to	Curator
Opening hours and facilities	10.30-1.00, Thur; photocopying
Guides	O.C. Goodbody, *Guide to Irish Quaker Records, 1654-1860* (Dublin, 1967)

Major collections
Quaker records, minute books, family lists, sufferings.
Testimonies of denial, disownments, 17th-20th century.
Letters and documents relating to relief work in the Great Famine.
Registers of births, marriages and burials, 17th-20th century.
Collections of letters, 18th-20th century.
Diaries; records of Quaker schools in Ireland; collection of photograph
     albums and scrapbooks. Museum items; samplers, embroidery, dress.
Pedigrees, wills, deeds, marriage certificates, 17th-20th century.
Pamphlets and correspondence related to Quaker mission and service.

113 Religious Society of Friends Ulster Quarterly Meeting

Address	Friends Meeting House, Railway St, Lisburn, Co. Antrim
Telephone	None
Enquiries to	Archives Committee
Opening hours and facilities	Postal enquiry only
Guides	O.C. Goodbody, *Guide to Irish Quaker Records, 1654-1860* (Dublin, 1967)

Major collections
Records of the Society of Friends in Ulster from 1673: minutes of meetings;
births, marriages and death records; sufferings.

114 Representative Church Body Library

Address	Braemor Park, Rathgar, Dublin 14
Telephone	(01) 979979

Enquiries to	Librarian & Archivist
Opening hours and facilities	9.00-1.00, 1.45-5.00, Mon-Fri; photocopying; photography; microfilming
Guides	J.B. Leslie, *Catalogue of manuscripts in possession of the Representative Church Body* (Dublin, 1938). Report of the Library & Records Committee (containing an annual accessions list) published annually in the *Journal of the General Synod of the Church of Ireland*. Church of Ireland parochial registers in the R.C.B. Library, Dublin published biennially in *The Irish Genealogist* (1982-).

Major collections

Church of Ireland archives: parochial, diocesan and cathedral records (principally from the Republic of Ireland) and records of the General Synod and the Representative Church Body, 13th-20th century.

Records of societies and organizations related to the Church of Ireland: schools, educational societies, missionary organizations, clerical groups, 18th-20th century.

Miscellaneous ecclesiastical manuscripts; papers of clergy and laity (correspondence, diaries, research notes and writings, scrapbooks, photographs); transcripts of and extracts from non-extant Church of Ireland records, 17th-20th century.

Microfilms of Church of Ireland records in other custodies, 17th-20th century.

115   Roscommon County Council

Address	Courthouse, Roscommon
Telephone	(0903) 26100 (ext. 113)
Enquiries to	Co. Secretary
Opening hours and facilities	By appointment; photocopying
Guides	Catalogue available at County Library, Abbey St, Roscommon

Major collections
Athlone: No. 2 Rural District Council minutes, 1899-1925.
Boyle: Board of Guardians minutes, 1883-1920; Dispensary District minutes, 1852-96; Rural District Council minutes, 1896-9; Rural District Council quarterly minutes, 1900-25.
Carrick-on-Shannon: Rural District Council minutes, 1903-16.
Castlerea: Board of Guardians minutes, 1839-1908; Rural District Council minutes: 1902-25.
Roscommon: Board of Health minutes: 1921-42; County Council minutes: 1899- ; Grand Jury records, 1818-99; Pension Committee minutes, 1908-51; Board of Guardian minutes, 1884-1921; Rural District Council minutes, 1899-1926; Town Commissioners minutes, 1873-1910.
Strokestown: Board of Guardians minutes, 1850-1913; Rural District Council minutes, 1899-1921.

116   Royal College of Physicians of Ireland

Address	6 Kildare St, Dublin 2
Telephone	(01) 616677
Enquiries to	Librarian
Opening hours and facilities	9.30-1.00, 2.00-5.00, Mon-Fri; July-Aug, check in advance; photocopying
Guides	None

Major collections
Complete series of College minute books, 1692- ; registers of fellows and members, late 17th century- ; Committee proceedings books, 1828- ; College correspondence, 1863- ; administrative records relating to the Library, 19th century.
Medical and Philosophical Society minutes, 1756-84, 1856-1939.
Dublin Sanitary Association minutes, late 19th century.
National Association for the Prevention of Tuberculosis minutes, late 19th century.
Cow Pock Institution subscription book, 1804-43.
Indian Hospital case books, late 19th century.

Westmoreland Lock Hospital records, 1792-1922.
Sir Dominick Corrigan (1802-1880): private papers.
   Kirkpatrick biographical file: information on some 10,000 Irish medical practitioners.
Sir Patrick Dun's Hospital records, 1808-1986.

117   Royal College of Surgeons in Ireland

Address   123 St Stephen's Green,
                  Dublin 2

Telephone   (01) 780200

Enquiries to   Sub-Librarian, Special Collections

Opening hours   9.15-5.00, Mon-Fri. Researchers are strongly advised to
and facilities write in advance; photocopying; photography

Guides   None

Major collections
Records created by the Royal College of Surgeons in Ireland, 1784- .
Records created by other institutions:
Mercer's Hospital (1734-1983): minute books of the governors 1736- ; minute
   books of the medical board; clinical records of various departments of the
   hospital;
The House of Industry Hospitals: minute books of the Corporation for
   relieving the poor in the County and City of Dublin, 1772-1871;
The Meath Hospital (founded 1753): sixteen volumes including governors'
   minute books, 1807- ;
The Surgical Society of Ireland: minutes of meetings of Council.
Records created by individuals associated with the history of medicine in
   Ireland: Richard Butcher, surgeon to Mercer's Hospital: case books,
   1846-59; Charles A. Cameron, College historian: diaries, 1880-1916;
   Abraham Colles, surgeon (1773-1843): documentation relating to Colles;
   William Doolin (1887-1962), surgeon and literary figure: papers; A.
   Jacob, President RCSI, 1837 and 1864: correspondence, 1840-3; Bethel
   Solomons, gynaecologist: case books, 1914-21; L.B. Somerville-Large,
   ophthalmologist: case books, 1902-10; J.D.H. Widdess, (1906-82),
   College librarian and historian: papers.

118 Royal Dublin Society

Address   Merrion Rd,
Ballsbridge,
Dublin 4

Telephone   (01) 680645

Enquiries to   Librarian-in-Charge

Opening hours 10.00-5.00, Tue, Fri, Sat; 10.00-7.00, Wed, Thur; archives
and facilities   available by arrangement only; photocopying

Guides   None

Major collections

Original minute books, 1731-64 (proceedings published from the minutes after 1764); Science Committee minute books, 1816-1979; Library Committee minute books, 1816-1984; Industries, Art and General Purposes Committee minute books, 1890- 1917; Fine Arts Committee minute books, 1816-89.

Private paper collections of Professor George Fitzgerald (School of Engineering, Trinity College Dublin), Dr Horace H. Poole, Richard M. Barrington and John Edmund Carew.

Records of the Radium Institute.

Photographic collection.

119 Royal Irish Academy

Address   19 Dawson St,
Dublin 2

Telephone   (01) 762570/764222

Enquiries to   Librarian

Opening hours 9.30-8.00, Mon (except Jul-Sept, closed at 5.30);
and facilities   9.30-5.30, Tue-Fri. The Library is closed for two weeks in
August; photocopying; photography; microfilming

Guides   Notes on Important Manuscripts in the Royal Irish
Academy. Catalogue of Irish Manuscripts in the Royal
Irish Academy.

Major collections:
Collection of manuscripts pre-1600 includes: the Cathach, 6th century; Domhnach Airgid, 8th century; Stowe Missal, 9th century; Lebor na hUidre, 12th century; Book of Ballymote, 14th century; Book of Lecan, Leabhar Breac, Book of Fermoy, Book of Hours and Austin Friars' Breviary, 15th century.
Collection of manuscripts in Irish, 17th-20th century, includes Annals of Four Masters.
Other collections include the records of the Ordnance Survey, antiquarian notebooks and sketches, genealogical papers (De La Ponce, Marquess MacSwiney, H.A.S. Upton), natural history papers (D.Y. Pack-Beresford, C.B. Moffat, R.A. Phillips, R. Lloyd Praeger), and members' papers (Lord Charlemont, O.J. Bergin, E. Knott).

120   Royal Society of Antiquaries of Ireland

Address	63 Merrion Square, Dublin 2
Telephone	(01) 761749
Enquiries to	Librarian
Opening hours and facilities	2.00-5.00, Mon-Fri. An appointment is advisable; photocopying
Guides	William Cotter Stubbs, 'The Weavers' Guild, the Guild of the Blessed Virgin Mary, Dublin 1446-1840', *Journal of Roy Soc of Antiquaries of Ireland*, xliv 1 (1919), 60-88

Major collections
Corporation books of Irish towns, especially from Co. Kilkenny; records of the Weavers' Guild of Dublin 1676-1840; archives of the RSAI, 1849- , (incomplete); a 13th century illuminated Sarum missal; topographical drawings including 12 volumes of sketches by George Victor du Noyer and 1 volume by George Miller; notebooks of Patrick Joseph O'Reilly (1854-1924), including transcripts of 1642 depositions, and 23 volumes of pedigrees of the O'Reilly's; papers of Francis Elrington Ball, 1863-1829, historian and antiquary; and the papers of Lord Walter Fitzgerald, 1858-1923, soldier and antiquary, founder and editor of the *Co. Kildare Archaeological Society Journal*.

121   Royal Ulster Rifles Regimental Museum

Address   RHQ The Royal Irish Rangers,
                 5 Waring St,
                 Belfast BT1 2EW

Telephone   (084) 232086

Enquiries to   Honorary Curator

Opening hours   9.00-4.00, Mon-Fri
and facilities

Guides   None

Major collections
Officers' records of service, 83rd and 86th regiments, 19th century (microfilm); recruits' registers, 1924-39; unit war diaries, World War I and World War II; medal rolls; photograph albums and scrapbooks, 1900- ; films.

122   St Canice's Cathedral Library

Address   St Canice's Cathedral,
                 Kilkenny

Telephone   (056) 21633

Enquiries to   Librarian

Opening hours   By appointment
and facilities

Guides   None

Major collections
Archives of the diocesan registrar of Ossory, Ferns and Leighlin, late 19th
     century- .
Miscellaneous papers of Lord John George Beresford, Archbishop of
     Armagh, relating to the dioceses of Ossory, Ferns and Leighlin, 1825- 42.

123 St Columb's Cathedral

Address	London St, Londonderry
Telephone	(080504) 262746
Enquiries to	The Dean
Opening hours and facilities	9.00-1.00, 2.00-5.00, Mon-Sat
Guides	Richard Hayes, *The Register of Derry Cathedral* . . . 1642-1703 (Dublin, 1910)

Major collections

Cathedral and parish records, 1642- .

Munn Collection: 32 volumes of copies of records relating to the history of the City and County of Londonderry, 17th-19th century.

Tenison Groves Collection: copies of records relating to Londonderry including valuable information on the history of the London Companies, 17th century- .

124 St Patrick's Cathedral, Dublin

Address	Dublin 8
Telephone	(01) 539472
Enquiries to	The Dean's Secretary
Opening hours and facilities	Postal enquiry/by appointment
Guides	None

Major collections

Cathedral muniments: deeds, rentals, accounts, legal papers, chapter and board minutes, election records, maps and drawings, correspondence, scrapbooks, 16th century- .

125   St Patrick's College, Maynooth

Address	Maynooth, Co. Kildare
Telephone	(01) 285222
Enquiries to	President
Opening hours and facilities	By arrangement only; photocopying
Guides	None

Major collections
Archives of the College, 1795- .
Archives of the Irish College at Salamanca and other Irish colleges in Spain;
  c. 50,000 documents, 1592-1936.

126   St Patrick's College, Maynooth
               Russell Library

Address	Maynooth, Co. Kildare
Telephone	(01) 285222
Enquiries to	Librarian, Special Collections
Opening hours and facilities	9.30-1.00, Mon-Fri. Researchers are advised to write or telephone in advance; photography
Guides	Paul Walsh, *Catalogue of Irish manuscripts in Maynooth College Library* (Ma Nuad, 1943). Padraig O Fiannachta, *Clar lamhscribhinni Gaeilge Mha Nuad*, fasc. 2-8 (Ma Nuad, 1965-73).

Major collections
12 volumes of Irish manuscripts copied for or collected c. 1820 by Dr John
  Murphy, Bishop of Cork (1771-1847); includes romances, religious and
  secular poetry, sermons, translations of devotional works, lives of saints
  and genealogies.

c. 100 Irish manuscripts collected by Eugene O'Curry (1796-1862), and additional material transcribed by him.

30 volumes of Irish manuscripts collected by Dr Laurence Renehan, President of the College (1845-57).

Illuminated manuscripts and books of hours; other manuscripts in Latin including: liturgical material, commentaries on scripture and canon law, and student notebooks from Douay and the Sorbonne.

Modern manuscript material in English including Dr Renehan's historical papers, Fr Shearman's genealogical papers, and the manuscript of 'The Master', a play by Patrick Pearse.

127 St Patrick's College, Thurles

Address Thurles,
Co. Tipperary

Telephone (0504) 21201/21822

Enquiries to Archivist

*Opening hours
and facilities* By appointment
photocopying

Guides None

Major collections

The College archives are composed mostly of College records and property documents. The historical notes compiled by Father Walter Skehan and Canon Philip Fogarty are retained in the College. These notes are an invaluable source for parochial histories of the archdiocese as well as containing important genealogical information. The College archives also contain other miscellaneous items such as Judge Keogh's notebook used at the trial of the Cormack brothers and some rentals of Thurles Estate.

128 St Peter's College

Address Summerhill,
Wexford

Telephone (053) 22071/22265

Enquiries to	President
Opening hours and facilities	By appointment and postal enquiry; photocopying
Guides	None

Major collections
Hore Manuscripts relating to the history of Wexford, c. 1798.
Material relating to the development of St Peter's College, 1811- .
Papers of Revd T. O'Byrne, G. Flood and R. Ranson.

129 Sisters of the Holy Faith

Address	Holy Faith Convent, Glasnevin, Dublin 11
Telephone	(01) 373427
Enquiries to	Archivist
Opening hours and facilities	Postal enquiry only; photocopying
Guides	None

Major collections:
Correspondence of founders, Margaret Aylward and Fr John Gowan CM, 1840s- . Life and lectures of Fr Gowan. Life and spiritual notes of John Joseph Steiner, a German convert and collector for St Brigid's Orphanage. Files relating to each convent of the Congregation including those in the Mission Fields. Aylward family papers. Personal effects of founders.

130 Sligo County Library

Address	The Courthouse, Sligo
Telephone	(071) 2212
Enquiries to	Co. Librarian

Opening hours and facilities	10.00-1.00, 2.00-5.00 Tue-Fri; photocopying
Guides	None

Major collections

Minute books of Board of Guardians, 1850-90; Grand Jury Presentments minute books, 1813-51 & 1877-99; Sligo Co. Council minute books, 1899-1950;

J.C. McDonagh MSS relating to Co. Sligo (22 vols).

Rentals of Palmerston Estate, 1860, 1879, 1888, 1902.

Pedigrees of various co. families.

Drawings of antiquities of Co. Sligo by W.F. Wakeham.

131   Sligo Harbour Commissioners

Address	Harbour Office, Sligo
Telephone	(071) 61197
Enquiries to	Secretary
Opening hours and facilities	By appointment only
Guides	None

Major collections

Minute books, 1824-8, 1847- ; memoranda of agreements book, 1823-92; miscellaneous accounts and operational books, late 19th century- ; report on improvements to harbour, 1822.

132 State Paper Office

Address	Dublin Castle, Dublin 2
Telephone	(01)792777 (ext. 2518)
Enquiries to	Keeper of State Papers
Opening hours and facilities	10.00-5.00, Mon-Fri; photocopying; photography; microfilming
Guides	An introductory leaflet, containing a summary of the main groups and classes of state papers, is available in this office. *Reports of the Deputy Keeper of Public Records in Ireland*, vols 1-59 (1869-1962) contain details of accessions to the State Paper Office and transfers of state papers to the Public Record Office. B. Mac Giolla Choille, 'Fenian documents in the State Paper Office', *Irish Historical Studies* vol xvi, no. 63 (March 1969). B. Mac Giolla Choille, *Intelligence Notes, 1913-16* (Stationery Office, Dublin, 1966). *The Rebellion of 1798* facsimile documents (1979). *Sources for local studies in the Public Record Office and State Paper Office* facsimile documents (1982). *Transportation, Ireland-Australia, 1798-1848* facsimile documents (1983).

Major collections

Records of the Chief Secretary's Office: Rebellion Papers, 1790-1807; Official Papers, 1790-1922; State of the Country Papers, 1790-1831; Registered Papers, 1818-1922.

Records of departments of the Chief Secretary's Office: Privy Council Office, 1800-1922; Convict department, 1778-1924; Chief Crown Solicitor's department, 1815-1922.

Police and Crime records: Irish Crimes records, 1848-93; Fenian Papers, 1857-83; Crime Branch Special records, 1887-1920.

Prison administration records: Government Prisons Office, 1836-80; General Prisons Board, 1877-1928.

Cabinet and Dáil Éireann records: Cabinet files and minutes, 1919-54; Dáil Éireann Secretariat files, 1919-22.

133 Stranmillis College Belfast

Address	Stranmillis Rd, Belfast BT9 5DY
Telephone	(084) 665271 (ext. 309)
Enquiries to	Librarian
Opening hours and facilities	9.00-5.00, Mon-Fri; enquirers are asked to write in advance; photocopying; photography
Guides	None

Major collections

Documentary and photographic records of the College and grounds since its establishment in 1922. Also prospectuses and other printed ephemera.

134 Strokestown Park House

Address	Strokestown Park, Co. Roscommon
Telephone	(078) 33013
Enquiries to	Curator
Opening hours and facilities	By appointment; postal enquiry
Guides	None

Major collections

Papers relating to Strokestown Park House and the Pakenham Mahon family. The greater part of these papers is in the National Library of Ireland.

Volume of estate maps for Sandford estate, Castlereagh.

Large collections of glass plates and early photographs, 19th century- .

135 Tipperary Joint Libraries

Address Castle Ave,
Thurles,
Co. Tipperary

Telephone (0504) 21555/21154/21102/21156

Enquiries to Local Studies Department

Opening hours 10.00-1.00, 2.00-5.30, Mon-Fri;
and facilities photocopying

Guides Introductory leaflet available in branch libraries

Major collections

Poor Law Union records: Borrisokane, 1850-1925; Cashel, 1844-1925; Clogheen, 1839-1929; Clonmel, 1839-1924; Nenagh, 1839-1924; Roscrea, 1839-1924; Thurles, 1839-1924; Tipperary, 1839-1923.

Presentments to the Grand Juries of Tipperary, 1842-99.

Rentals, maps, schedules relating to the sale of encumbered estates: lands in the barony of Slieveardagh/Comsy, 1851; estates of the Earl of Portarlington at Borrisoleigh, 1855 and Roscrea, 1858; estate of Viscount Chabot at Thurles and Thomastown, 1859.

Family papers: Coopers of Killenure, 1879-98; Ryans of Inch, 1650- 1928.

136 Tipperary South Riding County Museum

Address Parnell St,
Clonmel

Telephone (052) 21399 (ext. 349)

Enquiries to Curator

Opening hours 10.00-1.00, 2.00-5.00, Tue-Sat; by appointment;
and facilities photocopying

Guides An introductory leaflet and a series of interpretative lists and hand lists are available

91

Major collections
The County Museum holds an amount of archival material relating to local authorities in the county. It includes the minute books of Tipperary S.R. County Council, 1899-1952, and of various Council committees as well as the minute books of Fethard Town Commissioners, 1866-77, 1896-1929. The collections also include material relating to the Lismore estate and the records of the Republican Courts in the eastern part of the county during the War of Independence.

137 Trinity College, Dublin Geological Museum

Address	Geological Museum, Trinity College, Dublin 2
Telephone	(01) 772941 (ext. 1477)
Enquiries to	Curator
Opening hours and facilities	9.00-5.00, by appointment; photocopying; photography
Guides	None

Major collections
Geological Society of Dublin: minute book, 1850s- .
John Joly (1857-1933), geologist and physicist: correspondence, laboratory notebooks, diaries.
Louis B. Smyth (d. 1952), geologist: correspondence, laboratory notebooks, field notebooks, field maps.
R.G.S. Hudson (d.1963), geologist: correspondence.

138 Trinity College Library, Dublin Manuscripts Department

Address	College St, Dublin 2
Telephone	(01) 772941 (ext. 1189)
Enquiries to	Keeper of Manuscripts
Opening hours and facilities	10.00-5.00, Mon-Fri, 10.00-1.00, Sat; photography; microfilming
Guides	T.K. Abbott, *Catalogue of the Manuscripts in the Library of Trinity College, Dublin* (Dublin and London, 1900) is a general catalogue of accessions to 1900, continued after that date in typescript form. Introductory leaflet to the department is available throughout the Library. Sectional language catalogues have appeared in print, including T.K. Abbott and E.J. Gwynn, *Catalogue of the Irish Manuscripts in the Library of Trinity College, Dublin* (Dublin, 1921). Marvin L. Colker, *A Descriptive Catalogue of the Mediaeval and Renaissance Latin Manuscripts in the Library of Trinity College Dublin* is forthcoming. Peter Fox (ed.), *Treasures of the Library, Trinity College Dublin* (Dublin, 1986) discusses some of the major holdings.

Major collections

Corpus of medieval manuscripts, largely from the collection of James Ussher (died 1656), but also including the Library's greatest treasures, such as the Book of Kells, Book of Durrow and Book of Armagh.

College muniments, 16th-20th century; Roman inquisitorial records, 16th-18th century; Depositions of 1641; 1798 rebellion papers.

Family and private papers collections of William King (1650-1729), archbishop of Dublin; Earls of Donoughmore, 16th-20th century; Sir William Rowan Hamilton (1805-65), mathematician and astronomer; Michael Davitt (1846-1906), author and politician; John Dillon (1851-1927), politician; Robert Erskine Childers (1870-1922), author and politician; John Millington Synge (1871-1909), poet and dramatist; Thomas Bodkin (1887-1961), art historian and gallery director; Thomas MacGreevy (1893-1967), poet and gallery director; Denis Johnston (1901-84), playwright and journalist.

139 Ulster Folk & Transport Museum Library

Address   Cultra Manor,
Holywood,
Co. Down BT18 0EU

Telephone   (08487) 428428

Enquiries to   Librarian

Opening hours 9.00-5.00, Mon-Fri;
and facilities   photocopying; photography

Guides   None

Major collections
Byers Folklore Collection, c. 1900.
Committee on Ulster Folklife and Traditions notebooks, c. 1960.

140 Ulster Museum

Address   Botanic Gardens,
Belfast BT9 5AB

Telephone   (084) 668251

Enquiries to   Librarian, Department of Local History

Opening hours 10.00-12.45, 2.00-5.00, Mon-Fri. Prior appointment
and facilities   preferred; photocopying; photography

Guides   *Concise catalogue of the drawing, paintings & sculptures in the Ulster Museum* (Ulster Museum, 1986).
N. Fisher, 'George Crawford Hyndman's MSS', *Journal of Conchology*, xix (1931), 164.
R.S. Turner and others, *A List of the Photographs in the R.J. Welch Collection in the Ulster Museum, 1: Topography and History* (Ulster Museum, 1979), *2: Botany, Geology and Zoology* (Ulster Museum, 1983).

Major collections

Templeton MSS: c. 25 vols of MSS of John Templeton (1766-1825), botanist; including his journal, 1806-25, several volumes of an unpublished Irish flora illustrated by himself, records of mosses and ferns and a list of Irish shells.

Hyndman MSS: numerous notes by George C. Hyndman (1796-1868), Belfast marine biologist; also dredging papers, Belfast Bay, 1844-57.

Thompson MSS: several folders of notes and correspondence of William Thompson (1805-52), Belfast naturalist and author of *Natural History of Ireland*.

Welch MSS: c. 20 vols of personal and excursion diaries, natural history notes, memoranda and lists of negatives of Robert J. Welch (1859-1936), photographer and amateur naturalist.

Botany and Zoology Department: small but important collections, including notebooks of P.H. Grierson (1859-1952) on Mollusca and one letter of Dr Alexander Henry Halliday (?1728-1802) relating to insecta.

Local History Department: extensive archive of manuscript and printed material, including the Barber MSS (Rev. Samuel Barber of Rathfriland, United Irishman) and the Tennant Collection (Robert J. Tennant, early 19th century Liberal politician from Belfast).

Non-manuscript material: posters and other ephemera, chiefly playbills and programmes of Belfast theatres (c. 200-250 items).

Belfast and other locally printed books, pamphlets, chapbooks and broadsides (c. 500 items).

Hogg Collection: approx. 5,500 glass plate negatives plus many lantern slides, by A.R. Hogg of Belfast (1870-1939), covering topography, industry, commerce, social conditions and portraits.

Welch Collection: c. 6,000 glass plate negatives by R.J. Welch of Irish subjects, covering topography, industries, rural crafts, antiquities, geology, botany and zoology.

Historical and Topographic Collection: c. 1,000 negatives, modern and copied from old prints and negatives (constantly growing); a few other collections, large and medium-sized (uncatalogued or in process of being catalogued).

A growing collection of several hundred slides made in the field and from specimens and photographs.

Departments other than Local History keep their own specialized collections of negatives and slides.

Local History Department: c. 250 maps; c. 1,500 topographical drawings, paintings and prints; c. 250 portraits.

Art Department: c. 2,000 drawings and watercolors.

Botany and Zoology Department: various watercolours and drawings.

141 University College Cork Boole Library

Address	University College, Cork
Telephone	(021) 276871 (ext. 2282)
Enquiries to	Assistant Librarian, Special Collections
Opening hours *and facilities*	9.30-1.00, 2.15-5.00, Mon-Fri; early closing 4.30, July-Sept; photocopying;
Guides	P. de Brún, *Clár lámhscríbhinní Gaeilge Choláiste Ollscoile Chorcaí: cnuasach Thorna* (1967). B. O Conchuir, 'Scriobhaithe Chorcaí, 1700-1850', *An Clochomhar* (1982). P. Bull, 'William O'Brien MSS in the library of UCC', *JCHAS* lxxv (1970).

Major collections

Papers, mainly academic, of former presidents and professors including Tadhg O Donnchadha, Alfred O'Rahilly, M.D. MacCarthy, Cormac O Cuilleanain, Daniel Corkery, and G. Boole.

Kilsale manorial records, 17th century; minutes of Cork Cuvierian Society; Grehan family papers; records relating to the Seward estate in Youghal, 19th-20th century; miscellaneous papers of William O'Brien; literary works of Patrick Galvin.

Collections of Gaelic manuscripts of O Murchadha, de Paor, O Cathalain and O Leighinn.

Torna MSS including material collected and transcribed by him.

142 University College Dublin Archives Department

Address	Belfield, Dublin 4
Telephone	(01) 693244
Enquiries to	Archivist

Opening hours and facilities	9.30-4.30, Mon-Fri. Researchers are strongly advised to write in advance; photocopying; photography
Guides	A.C. Holland and S. Helferty (comps), *Guide to the Archives Department, University College Dublin* (1985)

Major collections

Archives of the College, 1909-66, and of predecessor bodies including the Catholic University, 1854-1911, the Royal College of Science for Ireland, 1867-1926, the Museum of Irish Industry, 1846-67, and the Albert Agricultural College, 1838-1926.

Private paper collections relating to the movement for national independence and the history and development of the modern Irish state. Major collections include the papers of Ernest Blythe, Michael Collins, the Cumann na nGaedheal and Fine Gael parties, Desmond FitzGerald, Michael Hayes, T.M. Healy, Hugh Kennedy, Sean MacEntee, Patrick McGilligan, Eoin MacNeill, Mary MacSwiney, Terence MacSwiney, Richard Mulcahy, Daniel O'Connell, Cearbhall O Dalaigh, Diarmuid O hEigeartaigh, Ernie O'Malley, Desmond Ryan, and Moss Twomey.

Trade union archives and labour-related private paper collections, deposited through the Irish Labour History Society. Includes archives of actors, bakers, coopers, municipal employees, plasterers, shoe and leather workers, and woodworkers trade unions, 1800-1980.

143 University College Dublin Roinn Bhéaloideas Éireann/ Department of Irish Folklore

Address	Belfield, Dublin 4
Telephone	(01) 693244
Enquiries to	Head of Department
Opening hours and facilities	2.30-5.30, Mon-Fri, excluding August; photocopying; photography; microfilming
Guides	Seán Ó Súilleabháin, *A Handbook of Irish Folklore* (Dublin 1942, Detroit 1970)

Major collections
Manuscripts, films, photographs, drawings and sound recordings held by the former Irish Folklore Commission (1935-71) as well as substantial additions, including video recordings, to these collections since 1971. The bulk of the manuscript holdings and sound and video recordings is in the Irish language, but these collections also contain large amounts of English-language material as well as smaller amounts of material in Scottish Gaelic and in the Manx and Breton languages.

144 University College Dublin Special Collections

Address	Library, University College, Belfield, Dublin 4
Telephone	(01) 693244 (ext. 7686)
Enquiries to	Special Collections Librarian
Opening hours and facilities	9.30-1.00, 2.30-5.30, Mon-Fri; annual closure in first two weeks of July. Researchers should write or telephone in advance; photocopying; photography; off-premises microfilming can be arranged
Guides	Introductory leaflet

Major collections
Some papers relating to the movement for national independence, Irish language and local history, and early 20th century Anglo-Irish literature.
Includes letters and papers of and relating to James Joyce (1882- 1941), Patrick Kavanagh (1904-67), Thomas Kettle (1880-1916), Henry Morris (Énrí Ó Muirgheasa) (1874-1945), John O'Donovan (1809-61), Seán Ó Ríordáin (1916-77), William Reeves (1815-92), Katherine Tynan (1861-1931) and Jack Butler Yeats (1871-1957).

145 University College Galway James Hardiman Library

Address	Manuscripts Section, James Hardiman Library, University College, Galway
Telephone	(091) 24411
Enquiries to	Assistant Librarian
Opening hours and facilities	9.30-5.00, Mon-Fri; advance notice advisable; photocopying
Guides	Published work on the Corporation MSS, can be found in Royal Commission on Historical Manuscripts, *10th Report* (1885), 380-520 and in various issues of the *Galway Archaeological & Historical Society Journal*. A calendar of the Eyre Deeds is published in the same journal.

Major collections

Galway City civic records, 1485-1818, 1836-1922, with supplementary material arising from research undertaken on them.

The Hyde MSS Collection, bequeathed by Douglas Hyde, containing volumes of prose, poetry and various tracts penned by scribes from the 18th century and including miscellaneous manuscripts of Douglas Hyde.

Manuscripts in the Irish language and items reflecting the Gaelic revival are included in collections such as the papers of Stiophán Bairéad, c. 1880-1920.

Collections of papers from various local estates of the nineteenth century, including an extensive collection of legal and personal papers from the estate of the Wilson Lynch Family of Belvoir, Co. Clare, c. 1860-1930.

Eyre Deeds, a collection of legal papers relating to properties in Galway, 1720-1857.

Microfilmed records of the Galway Harbour Commissioners, 1830-1968.

146 University of Ulster Library

Address   Coleraine,
                            Co. Londonderry BT52 1SA

Telephone   (080265) 4141

Enquiries to   Librarian

Opening hours   9.00-10.00, Mon-Fri, 9.30-1.00 Sat during term; 9.30-5.30,
and facilities   Mon- Fri during vacation. Special collections available
                            only until 5.00 or by arrangement; photocopying;
                            photography by arrangement

Guides   *Guide to the Libraries* (annual)

Major collections
Papers of George Shiels (1881-1949), playwright; Denis Johnston (1901-84),
    playwright and author; George Stelfox (1884-1972), naturalist; E. Norman
    Carrothers (1898-1977), botanist and railway engineer.
Headlam-Morley collection of World War I material.
Paul Ricard collection of World War II material.

147 Valuation Office

Address   6 Ely Place,
                            Dublin 2

Telephone   (01) 763211

Enquiries to   Secretary

Opening hours   9.30-12.30, 2.00-4.30, Mon-Fri;
and facilities   photocopying

Guides   None

Major collections
Griffiths Primary Valuation, c. 1852, for the Republic of Ireland with accom-
panying maps. Records of the Valuation List, 1852- , showing occupiers of
properties.

148 Vincentian Fathers (Congregation of the Mission)

Address	4 Cabra Rd, Dublin 7
Telephone	(01) 801926/886961
Enquiries to	Archivist
Opening hours and facilities	By arrangement; photocopying
Guides	T. Davitt CM, 'The archives of the Irish Province of the Congregation of the Mission', *Catholic Archives* 5 (1985)

Major collections
Material relating to the history of Irish Vincentians in Ireland, Britain, China and Nigeria; to personnel; to St Vincent de Paul; to the general history of the Vincentians and to prominent individual non-Irish Vincentians, 1833- . Includes notebooks, sermon books, account books, theses, correspondence and a collection of published work of Vincentian interest.

149 Waterford Corporation

Address	City Hall, The Mall, Waterford
Telephone	(051) 73501
Enquiries to	Assistant Town Clerk
Opening hours and facilities	9.00-12.45, 2.00-5.00, Mon-Fri
Guides	Index of archives prepared and deposited in City Hall, Municipal Library and Trinity College Library

Major collections
The Liber Antiquissimus 1365-1649; the Scroll of Richard II, c. 1390; the Royal Charters (20 items), 1449-1815; records of the Council, 1655-1984.

Records of the Urban Sanitary Authority, 1874-1911; Waterford and New
  Ross Port Sanitary Authority, 1904-49; Committees of the Corporation,
  1778-1945; Town Clerk, 1377-1984; Engineer's Office, 1834-1960; Estate
  Office, 1700-1970; Finance Office, 1796-1958.
Small and private collections.
Maps and plans.

150   Waterford County Council

Address	County Library H.Q., Lismore, Waterford
Telephone	(051) 54128
Enquiries to	Co. Librarian
Opening hours and facilities	9.00-5.00, Mon-Fri; photocopying
Guides	None

Major collections
Miscellaneous Rural District Council, Board of Guardians, Grand Jury and
County Council records, 19th century- .

151   Wesley Historical Society Irish Branch

Address	Aldersgate House, 13 University Rd, Belfast
Telephone	(084) 795762
Enquiries to	Hon. Archivist
Opening hours and facilities	By appointment; photocopying
Guides	*Bulletin* of the Wesley Historical Society (Irish Branch)

Major collections

Methodist Church in Ireland: Conference agenda and minutes as published, 1878- ; Wesleyan Conference minutes, 1752-1878; Primitive Wesleyan Methodist Conference, 1818-78.

Microfilms of Methodist registers of Northern Ireland circuits.

Miscellaneous: writings of Methodists (correspondence, diaries, scrapbooks), photographs and other illustrative material, late 18th-20th century.

152   Wexford Corporation

Address	Municipal Buildings, Wexford
Telephone	(053) 22611
Enquiries to	Staff Officer and Asst. Staff Officer
Opening hours and facilities	9.00-1.00, 2.00-5.00, Mon-Fri; photocopying
Guides	None

Major collections

Minutes of Wexford Corporation, 1776- .

Copies of title documents, 17th century- .

"Lacey Book" and map: record of Corporate Estate by Thomas Lacey, Borough Treasurer, 1854.

Charter, 1846.

153   Wexford County Library

Address	Abbey St, Wexford
Telephone	(053) 22211 (ext. 359)
Enquiries to	Co. Librarian
Opening hours and facilities	2.30-5.30, Tue; 10.00-5.30, Wed-Fri; photocopying

Guides   None

Major collections
Miscellaneous Co. Wexford estate papers: maps, rentals and sales of rentals, 1825-1908.
Wexford Harbour Board: minutes, accounts, cash books; transactions relating to registered ships, 1830-1907; ship arrivals and departures from Wexford Harbour 1831-9, 1904-22; log book for Pilot Boat, 1930-61; Light Ship records, 1919-29.
Specifications for St Ives Harbour, Cornwall, 1868.
Minute book of Primrose League Ardcandrisk Habitation No. 1084, 1886-96.
Wexford Tate School accounts, 1895 & 1897-1911.
Ferrycarrig Bridge: interest on Carrig Bridge debentures, 1823-72.
Photocopy of survey of the parishes of Clone, Kilbride, & Ferns, 16 May 1776.
Photocopy of miscellaneous letters of Colclough family, c. 1800 and a copy of a transcript of the Declaration of Charles II in relation to the Colclough estate.
Typed copy of Samuel Barber's notes on Enniscorthy in 1798.

154   Wicklow County Council Archives

Address   County Library,
                 Greystones,
                 Co. Wicklow

Telephone   (01) 874387

Enquiries to   Co. Librarian

Opening hours 11.00-1.00, 2.00-4.00, Mon-Fri;
and facilities photocopying

Guides   None

Major collections
Grand Jury Presentment; Wicklow Co. Council minutes; minutes of the Board of Guardians, 19th century.

155   Wicklow Harbour Commissioners

Address   North Quay,
Wicklow

Telephone   (0404) 67455

Enquiries to   Secretary

Opening hours   By appointment only;
and facilities   photocopying

Guides   None

Major collections
Minute books, 1897-1954; damp press letter books, 1908-27; harbour dues
and tolls, 1891-1965; account books, receipt books and pay orders,
1854-1970; correspondence, deeds, leases, maps and drawings.

Appendix

Institutions and organizations which are believed to hold archives but which did not respond positively to the questionnaire and for which sufficient detail could not be obtained to complete entries.

Achonry [R.C.] Diocesan Archives
Carlow County Council
Clonfert [R.C.] Diocesan Archives
Cloyne [R.C.] Diocesan Archives
Columban Sisters
Communist Party of Ireland
Dominican Sisters
Down, Dromore & Connor Diocesan Registry
Fianna Fail
Football Association of Ireland
Gaelic Athletic Association
Garda Siochana Museum
Grand Orange Lodge of Ireland
Irish Football Association
Kildare & Leighlin [R.C.] Diocesan Archives
Kilaloe [R.C.] Diocesan Archives
Knights of St Columbanus
Labour Party
Limerick [R.C.] Diocesan Archives
Lutheran Church
Meath [R.C.] Diocesan Archives

Monaghan County Council
Moravian Church
Muckross House, Killarney
National Maritime Museum
National University of Ireland
Presbyterian Historical Society
Presentation Sisters
Redemptorist Fathers
Roscrea Heritage Centre
Ross [R.C.] Diocesan Archives
Royal Hibernian Academy of Arts
Royal Zoological Society of Ireland
St Colman's College, Fermoy
St John's College, Waterford
St Kieran's College, Kilkenny
St Patrick's College, Drumcondra
Salvation Army
Society of the Sacred Heart
Tuam [R.C.] Diocesan Archives
Waterford & Lismore [R.C.] Diocesan Archives
Workers' Party

County Index

The numbers refer to the Directory number.

Subject Index

The numbers refer to the Directory number.

courts 35, 41, 77, 88, 92, 107, 136
crime and criminals 41, 132
    see also Convicts, Prisons and
        Prisoners
Customs and Excise 107, 109

deaths 47, 48, 49, 62, 112, 113
    see also Parish registers
deeds 27, 36, 43, 70, 73, 76, 88,
    111, 112, 124, 145, 155
diaries 13, 43, 51, 87, 112, 114,
    117, 121, 140
dioceses (Catholic) 4, 6, 9, 11, 16,
    24, 31, 34, 37, 40, 45, 68, 73,
    104, 110, 127
diocese (Church of Ireland) 32,
    43, 86, 106, 114, 122
dispensaries 44, 115
distilling, distilleries 21
drama 65, 71, 138, 146

education 15, 28, 55, 56, 107, 108,
    114
    see also Colleges; Schools;
        Universities
elections 13
engineering 118
estate papers 5, 13, 21, 30, 44, 51,
    57, 82, 88, 92, 97, 107, 108, 127,
    130, 135, 136, 138, 141, 145, 153
exports and imports 46, 75, 88

famine 112
Fenianism and Fenians 102, 132
flora
    see Botany
folklore 83, 139, 143
Franciscans 42
Freemasons 52
Friends, Religious Society of 112,
    113

Gaelic League 51
gardening 94
genealogy 5, 32, 36, 41, 47, 63,
    112, 119, 126, 127
geology 50, 137, 140
grand juries 29, 69, 71, 82, 115,
    130, 135, 150, 154
graveyards 26
Greek literature 14
guilds 36, 53, 120

harbour:
    see Ports and Harbours
health
    see Public Health
Hebrew language and literature
    14, 62
heraldry 12, 47
Holy Ghost Fathers 54
hospitals 18, 44, 77, 88, 100, 107,
    116, 117
housing 26
Huguenots 3

imports
    see Exports and Imports
India 1, 14
intelligence (military) 89
Irish abroad 1, 12
Irish Christian Brothers 59
Irish colleges (continental) 42, 125
Irish language manuscripts 42, 55,
    61, 93, 97, 119, 126, 138, 141,
    143, 144, 145
Irish language revival 8, 145
Irish Parliamentary Party 138
Irish Republican Army 89

Jesuits 61
Jews 62

judges 36, 142

Land League and Land War 87
landlordds and tenants 5, 13, 41,
    70, 76, 77, 155
lawyers 55, 56
libraries 3, 8, 13, 14, 36, 43, 44, 67,
    69, 71, 79, 81, 82, 85, 96, 97,
    100, 102, 106, 109, 112, 114,
    116, 117, 118, 122, 126, 130,
    135, 138, 141, 144, 145, 146,
    150, 153, 154
literary papers 21, 66, 78, 81, 97,
    109, 126, 138, 141, 144, 146
local government 13, 21, 25, 26,
    29, 30, 35, 41, 44, 67, 69, 70, 71,
    74, 77, 79, 82, 84, 85, 88, 90, 92,
    100, 108, 115, 120, 130, 135,
    136, 145, 149, 150, 152, 154
London companies 123

manors 5, 141
maps and surveys 13, 18, 25, 27,
    35, 43, 50, 63, 75, 76, 80, 103,
    107, 108, 119, 124, 134, 135,
    137, 140, 147, 149, 153, 155
marriages 10, 48, 49, 62, 111, 112,
    113,
medicine 116, 117
meteorology 81
Methodists 151
military history 5, 12, 121
mills 57, 85
Missionary Sisters of the Holy
    Rosary 91
missions (religious) 1, 18, 51, 54,
    61, 91, 114, 129, 148
money and currency 2, 7
monasteries 42, 51
monuments 101
municipal corporations

see Local Government
museums 5, 23, 27, 41, 53, 62, 66,
    72, 78, 80, 87, 90, 92, 94, 98,
    105, 121, 136, 137, 139, 140, 142
music 109
muster rolls 5

natural history 94, 98, 119, 140,
    146
navigation 13, 63
New Zealand 1

observatories 39
oriental manuscripts 3, 14
orphans and orphanages 18, 52,
    129

painting and painters 14, 28, 94,
    95, 96, 118, 138, 140
Papacy
    see Vatican, Papacy
papyri 14
parish registers (Catholic) 6, 10,
    16, 34
parish registers (Church of
    Ireland 10, 107, 114
Parliament (Irish): House of
    Lords 47
parliamentary journals 55
philosophy 42
photographs, photography 13, 18,
    23, 35, 43, 58, 61, 64, 65, 71, 72,
    73, 80, 87, 94, 105, 112, 114,
    118, 121, 133, 134, 140, 143, 151
physics 137
poetry and poets 78, 81, 126, 138,
    145
police 87, 132
political papers 23, 37, 42, 51, 97,
    107, 108, 132, 138, 142, 144
ports and harbours 22, 33, 38, 46,

74, 75, 88, 99, 101, 102, 131, 145, 153, 155
Presbyterian Church 5, 13, 21
prisons 82, 87, 107, 132
public health 44, 67, 70, 77, 84, 85, 88, 92, 100, 107, 115, 116, 149
public records 102, 107, 108, 132
Public Works 77, 101, 107, 131

Quakers: *see* Friends, Religious Society of

railways 20, 63, 82, 146
rate books 26, 77, 88, 92
relief works 35, 101, 107, 112
Repeal of the Union 37
rivers 13, 63, 77, 90
rugby football 64

St Patrick, Order of 47
schools 13, 18, 28, 41, 52, 59, 105, 108, 112, 114, 153
science 118, 142
ships and shipping 99, 107
Sisters of the Holy Faith 129
Sisters of Mercy 17, 18, 19
societies (learned) 8, 12, 81, 118, 120, 137, 151
Spain 125
sport 64, 90

surgeons and surgery 117

theatres 65, 140
theology 42
tithe applotment books 107, 108
topography 36, 103, 120, 140
trade unions 21, 90, 97, 107, 142
tramways 63
transports 20, 63, 139

United States of America 1
universities 37, 109, 137, 138, 141, 142, 143, 144, 145, 146

valuation (property) 26, 147
Vatican, Papacy 17, 91
Veto question 42
Vincentian Fathers 148

War of Independence 23, 72, 89, 136, 138, 142
weather
    see meteorology
West Indies 1
wills 13, 47, 73, 107, 108, 111, 112
World War I 121, 146
World War II 12, 89, 121, 146

zoology 140